SPECTRUM®

Writing

Grade 7

Published by Spectrum®
an imprint of Carson-Dellosa Publishing
Greensboro, NC

Spectrum®
An imprint of Carson-Dellosa Publishing LLC
P.O. Box 35665
Greensboro, NC 27425 USA

ISBN 978-0-7696-5287-0

04-152127811

Table of Contents Grade 7

Chapter 1 Writing Basics

Chapter 2 Expressive Writing

Chapter 3 Descriptive Writing

Chapter 4 Writing to Entertain

Table of Contents, continued

Chapter 5 Persuasive Writing

Chapter 6 Explanatory Writing

Chapter 7 Informational Writing

Chapter 1

Lesson 1 Main Ideas and Details

The main idea of a paragraph is what the paragraph is all about. In most paragraphs, the main idea is actually stated in the paragraph. That statement is the **topic sentence**. A topic sentence may be anywhere in a paragraph, but most often it is either the first sentence or the last.

> The bluebirds playing in my yard are a lovely sight. They are Eastern Bluebirds, and their bright feathers easily catch my eye. They seem always to appear in groups of two or three. I wonder if they are families or just "friends." They move about in such a lively way from ground to telephone wires and back. And the little chitter I hear almost sounds like laughter.

Write the topic sentence from the paragraph.

_____

_____

The other sentences include details that support, or tell about, the main idea. Write two details from the paragraph.

_____

_____

_____

_____

_____

_____

Lesson 1 Main Ideas and Details

Not all paragraphs have a topic sentence. Sometimes, writers leave it out. The paragraph still has a main idea, but the writer chooses not to state the main idea in the paragraph. Here is an example.

> I was awakened by a bird this morning. It wasn't the sweet little "chirp, chirp" that you read about in children's stories. It was the "squawk, squawk" of a crow. He was right outside my window and he was loud, let me tell you. Why did he choose my window? What was he squawking about? It was not a good start to my day.

What is the main idea of the paragraph above?

_____

How do you feel about birds? Choose one of these sentences as a topic sentence for a paragraph:

> I don't know anything about birds.

> I like watching birds.

> I would like to be a bird.

Now, write a paragraph in which you support your main idea with details. Remember to choose just one topic sentence. Decide whether you will put it at the beginning, in the middle, or at the end of the paragraph.

_____

_____

_____

_____

_____

_____

_____

_____

_____

_____

_____

Lesson 2 Staying on Topic

Normally, all of the details in a picture fit the main idea. The same should be true of a paragraph: all of the details should fit the main idea. In other words, each sentence must stay on topic. The following paragraph contains a sentence that is not on topic. Read the paragraph and underline the topic sentence. Then, draw a line through the sentence that does not support the topic sentence.

When I was a kid, I especially loved stories that had animals as characters. Mice were my favorite. The mice in our attic sometimes make noise at night. Their homes always captured my imagination. It seems they always had little chairs and tables, shelves full of food, and little dishes that they had "stolen" from the people in the house. Bottle caps were bowls and matchboxes were beds. I always hoped that the mice in our house had homes as nice as the ones in my stories.

Now, write your own paragraph about a mouse or another story you remember from your childhood. Remember to stay on topic. Stick to one main idea and make sure that all of your detail sentences support that main idea. When you are finished, underline your topic sentence.

_____

_____

_____

_____

_____

_____

_____

_____

_____

_____

_____

_____

_____

Lesson 3 The Writing Process

Writers follow a plan when they write. The steps they take make up the writing process. Following these five steps leads to better writing.

Step 1: Prewrite

This is the "thinking and discovering" stage. Writers might choose a topic, or they might list everything they know about a topic already chosen. They might conduct research and take notes. Then, writers may organize their ideas by making a chart or diagram.

Step 2: Draft

Writers put their ideas on paper. This first draft should contain sentences and paragraphs. Good writers keep their prewriting ideas nearby. There will be mistakes in this draft, but there is time to fix them later.

Step 3: Revise

Writers change or fix their first draft. They move ideas around, put them in a different order, or add information. They make sure they used clear words and that the sentences sound good together. This is also the time to take out ideas that are not on topic.

Step 4: Proofread

Writers usually write or type a neat, new copy. Then, they look again to make sure everything is correct. They look especially for errors in capitalization, punctuation, and spelling.

Step 5: Publish

Finally, writers make a final copy that has no mistakes. They are now ready to share their writing.

Lesson 3 The Writing Process

What does the writing process look like? Manuel used the writing process to write a paragraph about ocean life. His writing steps below are out of order. Label each step with a number and the name of the step.

Step ____: _____

The ocean has three distnict zones or habitats. Similar to habitats on dry land. Closest to shore is the shallows and the continental shelf. These most fertile areas teem with life. plant and animal life abound. Rivers bring nutrients, and sunlight penetrates the water for warmth and light.

Step ____: _____

The ocean has three distinct zones, or habitats. Closest to shore are the shallows and the continental shelf. These most fertile areas teem with life. Rivers bring nutrients, and sunlight penetrates the water to provide warmth and light. Plant and animal life abound.

Step ____: _____

Shoshone

The ocean has three distnict zones or habitats. Similar to habitats on dry land. Closest to shore is the shallows and the continental shelf. These most fertile areas teem with life. plant and animal life abound. Rivers bring nutrients, and sunlight penetrates the water for warmth and light.

Step ____: _____

Step ____: _____

The ocean has three distnict zones or habitats. Closest to shore are the shallows and the continental shelf. These most fertile areas teem with life. Rivers bring nutrients, and sunlight penetrates the water to provide warmth and light. plant and animal life abound.

Lesson 4 Audience

When Mrs. Prescott writes a worksheet for her first-grade students, does she use long sentences and complicated words? No. She uses words and sentences that are appropriate for her students; they are her audience. If Mrs. Prescott does not keep her audience in mind, they will not understand. In this case, they will not learn.

When Mrs. Prescott writes a letter to her students' parents, does she use the same short words and sentences that she uses with her students? Surely not. The parents are adults; they can understand more complicated words and sentences than her students can. If Mrs. Prescott were to use first-grade language for the parents, they would lose interest. Writers need to keep their audience in mind at all times.

> Writers need to consider these questions every time they write.
>
> What will my audience enjoy?
>
> What are they interested in?
>
> What will make them want to keep on reading?
>
> What do they already know?
>
> What will they understand?

Here is a note that Mrs. Prescott wrote for her students' parents. Did she keep her audience in mind?

> Dear Parents,
>   On Thursday, April 11th, our class will visit the Children's Museum. The museum has rooms where the children can learn about clocks, water, fossils, and racecars. We are looking forward to a very exciting day.

Did she keep her audience in mind? How can you tell?

_____

_____

_____

Lesson 4 Audience

Put yourself in Mrs. Prescott's place and think about the five questions on page 10. What else should Mrs. Prescott have told the parents? Ask yourself: What would parents want or need to know about a field trip that their 6-year-old child is taking? Make up additional details, if you need to.

_____

_____

_____

_____

_____

_____

Now, write an information sheet for Mrs. Prescott's students to help them prepare for the field trip to the Children's Museum. Include at least one sentence about each of the four "rooms" and what children might see or learn there. Make up details as needed. Remember to ask yourself the five questions on page 10 before you write.

_____

_____

_____

_____

_____

_____

_____

_____

_____

_____

_____

_____

_____

_____

Lesson 5 Write a Paragraph

Here is what you know about paragraphs.

- A paragraph is a group of sentences about the same topic.

- Each sentence in a paragraph stays on topic.

- The main idea of a paragraph is what the paragraph is all about.

- A paragraph's main idea is usually stated in a topic sentence. The topic sentence may fall anywhere in the paragraph.

- The first line of a paragraph is indented.

- Writers must consider the audience for which they are writing.

What is your idea of a great field trip? Where would you go? What would you do? What would you learn? List some details that would be part of your perfect, one-day field trip.

Details:

_____   _____

_____   _____

_____   _____

Review your list. Think about the order in which you want to present your details in a paragraph. If you wish, number them. Then, draft a paragraph about your idea of a terrific field trip. Your purpose is to convince a teacher that your idea is a good one.

_____

_____

_____

_____

_____

_____

_____

_____

_____

_____

_____

Lesson 5 Write a Paragraph

Read through your paragraph. Ask yourself these questions. If necessary, make changes to your paragraph.

Questions to Ask About a Paragraph
Does the topic sentence express the main idea? **Does each sentence support the topic sentence?** **Does each sentence express a complete thought?** **Are the ideas in the paragraph appropriate for the audience?** **Is the first line indented?**

Now that you have thought about the content, or meaning, of your paragraph, proofread it for errors. Look through several times, looking for a certain kind of error each time. Use this checklist.

_____ Each sentence begins with a capital letter.

_____ Each sentence ends with the correct punctuation (period, question mark, or exclamation point).

_____ Each sentence states a complete thought.

_____ All words are spelled correctly.

Now, rewrite your paragraph. Use your neatest handwriting and make sure there are no errors in the final copy.

_____

_____

_____

_____

_____

_____

_____

_____

_____

_____

_____

Chapter 2

Lesson I Personal Narrative

Have you ever written a true story about something that happened to you? You were writing a personal narrative. A personal narrative is a true story an author writes about his or her own experiences. Read Nick's personal narrative.

After the Storm

It was a weird July day because it was so windy. It seemed more like a wild, November wind, except that it was warm. In mid-afternoon, it got calm. An hour later, a terrific thunderstorm swept through. The wind picked up again and really whipped the trees around. My brother and I watched out the windows.

After the storm, and after a cold supper, Mom said she had to go grocery shopping. "There's no food in the house, and your aunt is coming tomorrow," she said. Well, it looked to me as if there were food in the house, but there are some things that you just don't say to your mother. So, we all went to the grocery store.

The power was still out all over the neighborhood. We started to wonder whether the store would be open. But Mom said surely they had a generator. When we pulled into the parking lot, we saw that she was right. There were lights on in the store.

As soon as we stepped into the store, though, we realized that only about half of the store's lights were on. There was plenty of light to see by, but it wasn't the brighter-than-day light that grocery stores usually offer. And something else was weird, too. It was completely quiet. All of the fans and blowers were off. There was total silence in the store.

Mom, Pete, and I looked at each other. It didn't seem right to talk in such a quiet place. I felt as if I should tiptoe. I saw Mom wince when the grocery cart wheels squeaked.

There were just a few other people in the store. That was weird, too, because usually it's a pretty busy place. When we did talk, our voices sounded funny without all the background noise. The funny thing is, I had never even noticed the background noise. Was my entire life full of background noise that I never noticed?

Ever since then, I have been trying to listen to what is going on around me. When I'm outside, I hear barking dogs or distant traffic and maybe even some birds. When I'm inside, I hear fans and blowers, beeping cash registers, and crying babies. But at least I'm listening.

Lesson 1 Personal Narrative

Some people write personal narratives because they want to share their thoughts and feelings. Some write because they want to entertain their readers. Some might want to do both. As always, writers of personal narratives keep their audience in mind. What do they want to share with those readers?

Here are the features of a personal narrative:

- It tells a story about something that happens in a writer's life.

- It is written in the first person, using words such as *I, me, mine,* and *my.*

- It uses time and time-order words to tell events in a sequence.

- It expresses the writer's personal feelings.

What could you write a personal narrative about? Here are some idea-starters.

the quietest place you've been   the noisiest place you've ever been
a most exciting event   a most embarrassing moment
the funniest thing you ever saw   the busiest place you've ever been

What memories popped into your head as you read these idea-starters? Write some notes about each memory. One of these could be the start of a great personal narrative!

Idea-starter: _____

_____

Idea-starter: _____

_____

Idea-starter: _____

_____

Idea-starter: _____

_____

Idea-starter: _____

_____

Idea-starter: _____

_____

Lesson 2 Sequence of Events

In a personal narrative, writers need to tell when things happen and in what order. Using **time-order** words helps readers understand events and why they happen. Think of some time-order words or phrases. List them below. The list is started for you.

dawn	sunrise	today
Monday	next week	last night

_____

_____

_____

Now, use some of the time-order words you listed. Write a sentence that could be from a personal narrative. Use a time-order word or phrase at the beginning of your sentence.

_____

_____

_____

Write a sentence about something you did last week. Use a time-order word or phrase in the middle or at the end of your sentence.

_____

_____

_____

Lesson 2 Sequence of Events

In addition to time-order words, **transition** words help readers know when things happen and in what order. Here are some common transition words.

after	as soon as	before	during	finally	first
later	meanwhile	next	so	soon	then	when

Here is a paragraph from Nick's personal narrative on page 14. Circle the transition words when you find them.

> After the storm, and after a cold supper, Mom said she had to go grocery shopping. "There's no food in the house, and your aunt is coming tomorrow," she said. Well, it looked to me as if there were food in the house, but there are some things that you just don't say to your mother. So, we all went to the grocery store.

Think about a time when you were in a very quiet or a very noisy place. Where were you? What happened? What did you think about? Write the sequence of events in a paragraph. Remember that it is important to use time and time-order words, but don't start every sentence with a transition word. Use different sentence styles to keep your writing interesting.

_____

_____

_____

_____

_____

_____

_____

_____

_____

_____

_____

_____

_____

_____

_____

Lesson 3 Active Voice

Usually, the subject of a sentence does the action. That is easy to see in this sentence:

> The wind blows.

The verb in the sentence is an **active verb** because the subject (*wind*) does the action (*blows*).

What about this sentence?

> The tree was blown down.

Tree is the subject of the sentence. Does the tree do the action? No, the tree does not do the action; the tree "receives" the action. The verb, *was blown*, is a **passive verb** because the subject does not do the action.

Passive verbs are always two-part verbs. There is always one of these helping *verbs—am, is, was, be, been—*plus a main verb. However, that does that mean that whenever you see one of those helping verbs, you are looking at a passive verb.

> Passive verb: My bike *was tipped* over.

> Active verb: The wind *was blowing*.

How can you tell the difference? Ask yourself these two questions:

> What is the subject?

> Is the subject doing the action?

If the answer to the second question is "no," then you have a passive verb.

Sometimes, writers have to use passive verbs when they write. Maybe the writer doesn't know who did the action, so, "My bike was tipped over" is the only option. Most of the time, however, writing is clearer and more interesting if writers use active verbs.

Lesson 3 Active Voice

Compare these two paragraphs. The one on the left is written mostly with passive verbs. The one on the right is written with active verbs. What do you notice?

Residents were left with a clean-up job after the area was swept by strong thunderstorms and high winds yesterday afternoon. A severe weather warning was issued by the National Weather Service at 2:30 p.m. Within half an hour, reports of fallen trees and broken electrical lines were being called in by homeowners. Wind gusts of up to 65 miles per hour were recorded at the airport. In addition to fallen trees, many smaller branches and limbs were blown down by the storm. It was announced by the mayor that storm debris will be picked up by city crews starting tomorrow.

Strong thunderstorms and high winds that swept the area yesterday afternoon left residents with a clean-up job. The National Weather Service issued a severe weather warning at 2:30 p.m. Within half an hour, homeowners were calling in reports of fallen trees and broken electrical lines. The airport recorded wind gusts of up to 65 miles per hour. In addition to fallen trees, the storm blew down many smaller branches and limbs. The mayor announced that city crews will pick up storm debris starting tomorrow.

Underline the subject of each sentence below. Put an **X** next to each sentence that contains a passive verb.

_____ Nick was watching the storm.

_____ The sky was lit up by lightning.

_____ The yard was littered with branches.

_____ Pete was amazed.

Practice writing sentences with active verbs. First, look at the sentences above that have passive verbs. Rewrite one of those sentences with an active verb.

_____

Now, write a new sentence about a thunderstorm. Make sure you use an active verb.

_____

Lesson 4 The Writing Process: Personal Narrative

A personal narrative can be about the day you tamed a lion. However, if you've never done that, your personal narrative might be about something a little more normal. Remember the narrative you read on page 14? Nick wrote about going to the grocery store. There was nothing dangerous or exciting there. It was just an event that caused Nick to think a little bit. Follow the writing process to develop a personal narrative about an event in your own life. How did it change you?

Prewrite

Look again at the idea-starters on page 15 and the notes you made. Choose one of those ideas, or another idea that you like, and begin to explore it here.

My idea: _____

Use this idea web to collect and record details. Write down as many as you can.

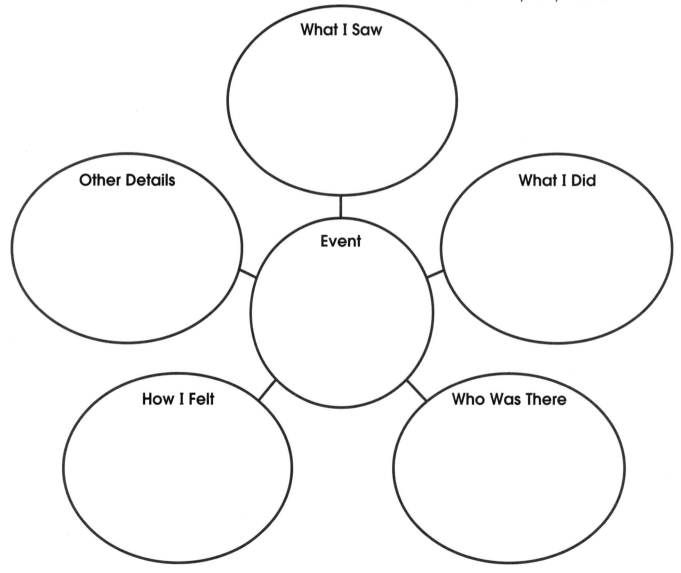

Lesson 4 The Writing Process: Personal Narrative

So far, you have chosen a topic and collected ideas. Now it is time to put your ideas in order. Think about the "story" you are about to tell in your personal narrative. Use the sequence chart on this page to list the events in order. Don't worry about details here; just put the events in order.

Lesson 4 The Writing Process: Personal Narrative

Draft

Write a first draft of your personal narrative on this page. Continue on another sheet of paper if you need to. Look back at your sequence chart on page 21 to help keep your ideas in order. As you write, don't worry about getting every word just right. Write your ideas in sentences and in order.

_____

_____

_____

_____

_____

_____

_____

_____

_____

_____

_____

_____

_____

_____

_____

_____

_____

_____

_____

_____

_____

_____

Write an idea for a title here.

Title:_____

Lesson 4 The Writing Process: Personal Narrative

Revise

One of the hardest things for any writer to do is to edit his or her own work. However, even experienced, professional writers know that they can almost always improve their first drafts. Improve your own first draft by answering the questions below. If you answer "no" to any questions, those are the areas that might need improvement. Make notes on your draft about changes you might make later.

- Did you tell about just one event or one "thing" in your narrative?
- Did you include details to make readers feel as if they are right there with you?
- Did you tell events in order? Did you use transition and time-order words to show when events happened?
- Did you tell how you felt about the events? Do readers get a sense of your personal feelings?
- Did you use active verbs?
- Does your story flow well when you read it out loud?

Now, focus on making sure you included details that will keep your readers interested. Did you use fantastic descriptive words, vivid verbs, and precise nouns?

When Nick revised his personal narrative, he added some descriptive words and phrases. Here is how Nick changed his opening paragraph.

It was a weird July day. ^because it was so windy/ It seemed more like a wild, November day ^windy, except that it was warm. In mid-afternoon, it got calm. ^An hour Later, a terrific thunderstorm swept through. The wind picked up again and really ^whipped blew the trees around. My brother and I watched out the windows.

Lesson 4 The Writing Process: Personal Narrative

Write the revision of your first draft. As you revise, remember to keep readers interested by using vivid descriptive words.

_____

_____

_____

_____

_____

_____

_____

_____

_____

_____

_____

_____

_____

_____

_____

_____

_____

_____

_____

_____

_____

_____

Now that you have revised your draft, are you still happy with your title? If not, write a new title here.

Title: _____

Lesson 4 The Writing Process: Personal Narrative

Proofread

Now it is time to correct those last errors. As you proofread, read for just one kind of error at a time. Read through once for capital letters, once for end punctuation, and once for spelling. Here is a checklist to help you proofread your revised narrative.

> ____ Each sentence begins with a capital letter.
>
> ____ Each sentence ends with the correct punctuation (period, question mark, or exclamation point).
>
> ____ Each sentence states a complete thought.
>
> ____ All words are spelled correctly.

When proofreaders work, they use certain symbols. Using these symbols makes their job easier. They will make your job easier, too.

Use these symbols as you proofread your personal narrative. Also, read your writing out loud. You might catch a mistake that you overlooked before.

- <u>c</u>apitalize this letter.
- Add a missing end mark: ⊙ ? !
- Add a comma please.
- Fix incorrect or misspelled words.
- "Use quotation marks correctly," she reminded.
- ~~Delete~~ this word.
- Lowercase this Letter.

Publish

Write or type a final copy of your personal narrative. If you wish, make a cover for it. You could even mount and display photographs to go along with your narrative. Double-check one last time for errors.

Chapter 3
Lesson 1 Sensory Details

In a description, a writer's goal is to help readers see, hear, smell, feel, or taste what is being described. Writers use **sensory details**, or details that appeal to readers' senses, in their description.

> I went to one of those mega-stores the other day. You know, the kind that has groceries on one side and everything else ever invented on the other. In spite of the fact that neon signs hang from the ceiling about every five feet, I was lost the minute I stepped in. I wandered around so long looking for a yellow wastebasket for my bathroom that I got hungry. Fortunately, a spicy scent led me to the café. After a grilled chicken sandwich and a tall, cold glass of sweet iced tea, I was ready for more wastebasket hunting. A whining, whirring sound told me an employee was approaching on a scooter. As she changed her mind, though, her back-up beeps faded down aisle 37, and there was my wastebasket. Success at last, and it took only three hours!

The sensory words, *whining* and *whirring*, for example, help you hear the scooter. What other sensory details does the paragraph contain? List them here, according to whether the detail helps you see, hear, smell, feel, or taste what is being described. Some details might fit into more than one category.

See: _____ _____ _____

Hear: _____ _____ _____

Smell: _____ _____ _____

Touch: _____ _____ _____

Taste: _____ _____ _____

Lesson 1 Sensory Details

Think of a store in which you have shopped. Was it a huge grocery store? Or was it a small shop full of scented candles? What was it like? Imagine yourself in the store. Can you describe the experience so that a reader feels as if he or she is right there?

First, record the sights, sounds, smells, textures, and flavors (if there were any) you experienced at the store.

Sights:_____ _____ _____

Sounds: _____ _____ _____

Smells: _____ _____ _____

Textures: _____ _____ _____

Flavors: _____ _____ _____

Now, put your words to work. Describe what it is like to be in this store. Appeal to all five of your readers' senses.

_____

_____

_____

_____

_____

_____

_____

_____

_____

_____

_____

_____

_____

_____

_____

_____

_____

_____

_____

_____

Lesson 2 Adjectives and Adverbs

To make a complete sentence, it takes just one noun and one verb.

Bands march.

Adjectives and adverbs describe, or modify, the words in a sentence to add interest or detail.

Adjectives modify nouns or pronouns. They tell *what kind*, *how much* or *how many*, and *which ones*.

Adverbs modify verbs, adjectives, or another adverb. They tell *how*, *when*, *where*, or *to what degree*. Many adverbs end in *ly*, but some do not, such as *not*, *never*, and *very*.

Adjectives at Work

This sentence contains no adjectives.

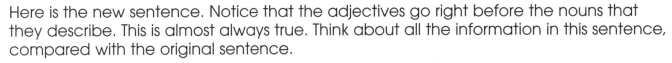

The bands march in the parade.

What kind of bands are they? They are high school bands.

How many bands are there? There are five of them.

What kind of parade is it? It is a Founder's Day parade.

Which Founder's Day parade? It is "our" Founder's Day parade.

Here is the new sentence. Notice that the adjectives go right before the nouns that they describe. This is almost always true. Think about all the information in this sentence, compared with the original sentence.

Five high school bands march in our Founder's Day parade.

Look at the sentences below. Think of at least two adjectives to add to each, then write the new sentence. Remember, an adjective tells more about a noun or pronoun.

A tuba player dropped his tuba.

_____

The flute player played her notes.

_____

A drummer kept beat with her mallets.

_____

Lesson 2 Adjectives and Adverbs

Adverbs at Work

Now, notice how some adverbs liven up a basic sentence.

>   The bands march in the parade.

How do they march? They march smartly.

When do the bands march? They always march.

To what extent do they march? They march "nearly" always.

Here is our new sentence. Notice that one adverb comes several words before the verb it describes. The other falls right after its verb.

>   The bands nearly always march smartly in the parade.

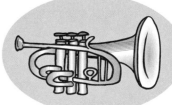

Look at each sentence below. Ask yourself whether you can add information about *how, when, where,* or *to what degree* with an adverb. Write your new sentence on the line.

A tuba player dropped his tuba.

_____

The flag-bearers waved their flags.

_____

Look at how both adjectives and adverbs work in this sentence.

>   tired   bravely   low
> The ˄tuba players ˄played their ˄notes.

Improve each sentence by adding one adjective and one adverb to make the sentence more vivid.

Marching in a parade can be tiring.

_____

Carrying a drum must be hard.

_____

The crowd loves the band.

_____

Lesson 3 Spatial Organization

When you walk into a room, you naturally look around in an organized way. You scan the room from left to right, up to down, or near to far, depending on the size or shape of the room, what is in the room, or what is happening in the room.

When writers describe a room or some other place, they must describe it in an organized way. This organization helps readers "see" the place just as if they were looking at it themselves. In the description below, Nina describes her sister's bedroom from near to far.

As you step into Shannon's room, you are engulfed by knee-high stacks of books and magazines. A narrow path leads forward. Should you take that path, you would find yourself in the middle of the room. To the left is an open closet door. The door is open because it is blocked by books. Inside are clothing and more books, of course. To the right is a bed. It is a rumpled island in a sea of books. At the far end of the room is a window. A curtain made out of book jackets blocks the late afternoon sun.

When we organize ideas by space, we use words that tell us where things are. Here are some common spatial words.

above	across	beside	between	beyond	into	left
low	middle	next to	over	right	through	under

Find these, or other spatial words, in the paragraph above. Circle them.

Look at the room around you. Write a paragraph to tell where some things are. Use spatial words in your sentences. The first sentence is started for you.

Next to me is _____

_____

_____

_____

_____

_____

_____

_____

_____

Lesson 3 Spatial Organization

Nina described her sister's cluttered bedroom. What kind of a cluttered place have you seen? It might be a store, a yard that you drove past, or your own bedroom! Describe the place. Choose a method of organization that makes sense. Use sensory details so that readers can see, hear, smell, and feel the view. Remember to use spatial words to tell where things are.

_____

_____

_____

_____

_____

_____

_____

_____

While sightseeing recently, imagine that you came across this building. Describe it for a friend back home. Organize the details of your description from top to bottom or from bottom to top.

_____

_____

_____

_____

_____

_____

_____

_____

_____

_____

Lesson 4 Describing Objects

When a writer describes an object, readers should be able to see, hear, smell, feel, and perhaps taste it. Can you describe something so vividly that your readers feel as if they are right there seeing it or holding it?

Take a close look at a familiar object that is nearby. Perhaps it's a pen, a pencil sharpener, or a classroom poster. Look at it as if you are seeing it for the first time. Write its details here.

Color: _____

Shape: _____

Size: _____

Texture: _____

Smell: _____

Other details: _____

Now, write a paragraph in which you describe the object. Again, describe it as if you are not familiar with the object. Remember to appeal to as many of your readers' senses as you can.

_____

_____

_____

_____

_____

_____

_____

_____

_____

_____

_____

_____

_____

_____

Lesson 4 Describing Objects

Now, choose a more complex object. Maybe it's an entire wall of the room you are in, or maybe it's a desk full of papers and books. Examine it. Even though it is a familiar object, look at it with fresh eyes. Record details of the object here.

Color: _____

Shape: _____

Size: _____

Texture: _____

Smell: _____

Other details: _____

Now, write a description of the object. Remember to organize your details logically in a side-to-side or top-to-bottom format.

_____
_____
_____
_____
_____
_____
_____
_____
_____
_____
_____
_____
_____
_____
_____
_____
_____
_____
_____
_____
_____
_____

Lesson 5 The Language of Comparison

To compare two things, use the ending **-er** or the word *more* to talk and write about how the two things are different.

For short words, such as *old*, add an **-er** ending.

> The first bike is *older than* the second bike.

For words that end in **y**, change the **y** to **i**, then add **er**.

> The second bike is *fancier than* the second bike.

For some one-syllable words, such as *fat*, double the final consonant, then add **er**.

> The new bike's tires are *fatter than* the old bike's tires.

For longer words, such as *expensive*, use *more* to compare.

> Which bike do you think is *more expensive*?

Do some more comparing. Look at the pictures and compare them. Use comparative forms of the words in the box to complete each sentence below.

big dangerous	scaly soft

The alligator is _____ than the rabbit.

If you touch the rabbit, it will surely be _____ than the alligator.

The alligator's skin would be much _____ than the rabbit's.

It would be _____ to meet an alligator than to meet a rabbit.

Lesson 5 The Language of Comparison

To talk or write about how three or more things are different, use the ending -**est** or the word *most*.

The unicycle bike is the *oldest* of the three bikes.

The yellow bike still has the *sportiest* design.

The yellow bike's tires are the *thinnest* of all.

The unicycle would be the *most expensive* of these three bikes.

The same spelling changes that occur when you add **er** to a word occur when you add **est** to a word. If you need to, look back at the bulleted list on page 34.

Take your turn comparing three objects. Look at the pictures. Then, use the words in the box to compare them.

energetic	messy
high	tame

_____

_____

_____

_____

_____

_____

Lesson 6 Comparing Objects

A Venn diagram is a tool that helps us compare things. In the diagram below, Chance compares his family's automobiles, a car and a truck.

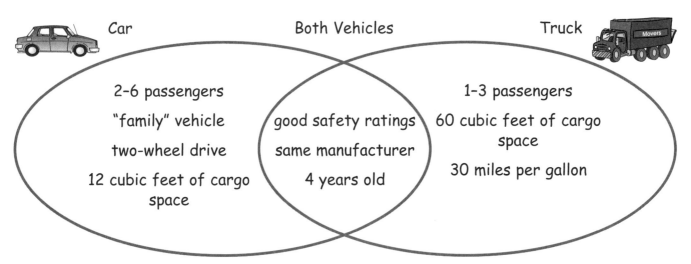

Car   Both Vehicles   Truck

2-6 passengers

"family" vehicle

two-wheel drive

12 cubic feet of cargo space

good safety ratings

same manufacturer

4 years old

1-3 passengers

60 cubic feet of cargo space

30 miles per gallon

To practice using a Venn diagram, compare a television with a computer. Record how each item is different. Then, write what is the same about each item.

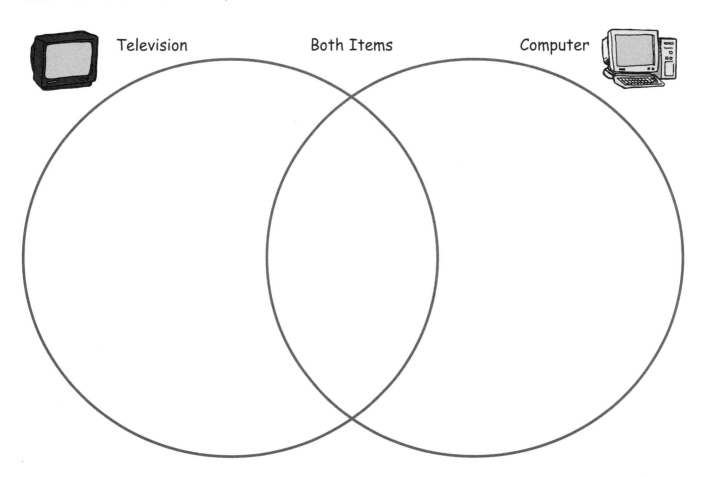

Television   Both Items   Computer

Lesson 6 Comparing Objects

Once you organize ideas in a Venn diagram, you can more easily write about those ideas. When writers write to compare, they must present information in a way that makes sense to readers. There are two ways to organize a written comparison. One way is to talk first about one object, then about the other. This is called a **whole-to-whole comparison**. Here is an example. Information about an apple is in red. Information about a banana is in black.

The apple's skin is smooth and shiny and may be eaten or pared off with a sharp knife. It is deep red, except near the stem, where the red fades to pink. The crisp flesh of the apple is juicy and sweet. The banana's thick peel is not edible, but peels off easily by hand. The yellow color is even from end to end. Inside, the banana's flesh is firm but not crisp. It is never juicy, and has a sweet tang that is like nothing else.

The other way is to talk first about one feature, or characteristic, as it relates to both objects. Then go on to another feature, and so on. This is a **part-to-part comparison**. Here is an example. Again, information about the apple is in red; information about the banana is in black.

The apple's skin is smooth and shiny and may be eaten or pared off with a sharp knife. The banana's thick peel is not edible, but peels off easily by hand. The apple is deep red, except near the stem, where the red fades to pink. The yellow color of the banana is even from end to end. The crisp flesh of the apple is juicy and sweet. The banana's flesh is firm but not crisp. It is never juicy, and has a sweet tang that is like nothing else.

Now, look back at the details you recorded on page 36 about a television and a computer. Write a paragraph in which you compare the two items. Decide which method of organization you will use: whole-to-whole or part-to-part. Then, write the paragraph. If you wish, use two different colors as you write.

_____

_____

_____

_____

_____

_____

_____

_____

_____

Lesson 7 Comparing Characters

When you read, it is only natural to compare a book you are reading with other books you have read. You may note how situations or characters are alike or different. Comparing characters, whether within a book or among different books, can help you understand a story and its developments.

You already know how to compare things with the help of a Venn diagram. Juyong made a diagram in her reader response journal to record what she knows so far about two characters in a book her class is reading.

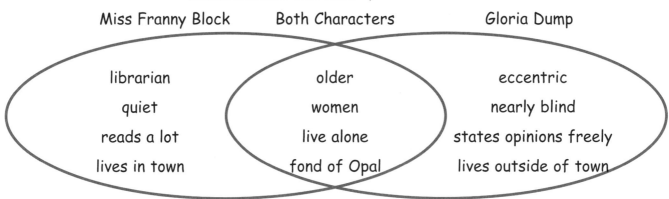

Because of Winn-Dixie by Kate DiCamillo

Miss Franny Block	Both Characters	Gloria Dump
librarian	older	eccentric
quiet	women	nearly blind
reads a lot	live alone	states opinions freely
lives in town	fond of Opal	lives outside of town

Think of characters in a book you are reading or have read lately. How are they alike and different? Fill out this Venn diagram with what you know about the characters. Think about how the characters act, or respond to what happens to them. Remember to label the circles with the characters' names.

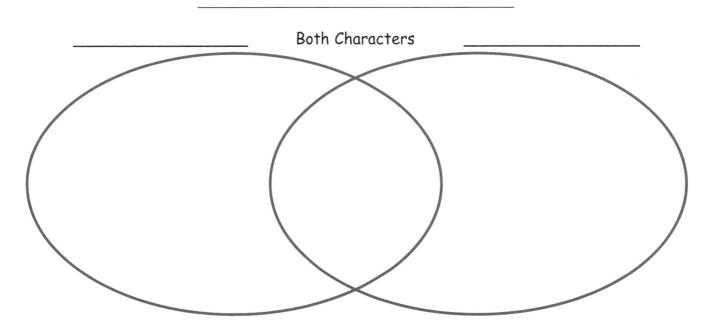

_____

_____ Both Characters _____

Lesson 7 Comparing Characters

Juyong's teacher has asked the students to write about Miss Franny Block and Gloria Dump, the characters from the book. Juyong reviews her Venn diagram, then chooses whole-to-whole organization for her paragraph. In other words, she'll talk about first one woman, then about the other.

Miss Franny is a typical librarian. She is a "very small, very old woman with short gray hair." She speaks politely and correctly and loves being a librarian. She is very proud of her library, which her father built for her in town.

Gloria Dump is "old with crinkly brown skin." She is nearly blind, and she has to put her false teeth in to eat. Gloria is sure to speak her mind, and states her opinions freely. She lives on the edge of town in a house with a wild and overgrown yard.

Now, review your own Venn diagram on page 38 and write about your two characters. Decide whether you will use whole-to-whole organization, as Juyong did, or part-to-part. Look back on pages 36 and 37 to review the two methods if needed.

_____
_____
_____
_____
_____
_____
_____
_____
_____
_____
_____
_____
_____
_____
_____
_____
_____
_____
_____

Lesson 8 The Writing Process: Descriptive Writing

Descriptive writing plays a role in many forms of writing. You see it in stories, in textbooks, and in newspaper articles. Use the writing process to develop a paragraph that describes a character you might include in a story.

Prewrite

Suppose you are trying to describe a person to someone who has never met that person. Think about how the person looks, moves, acts, and talks. First, think of some types of characters that you might like to write about. List them below:

_____   _____

_____   _____

_____   _____

Now, look over your list. Which character seems most appealing? Choose one and write the character's name here.

Character I will describe: _____

Use this idea web to record details about your character.

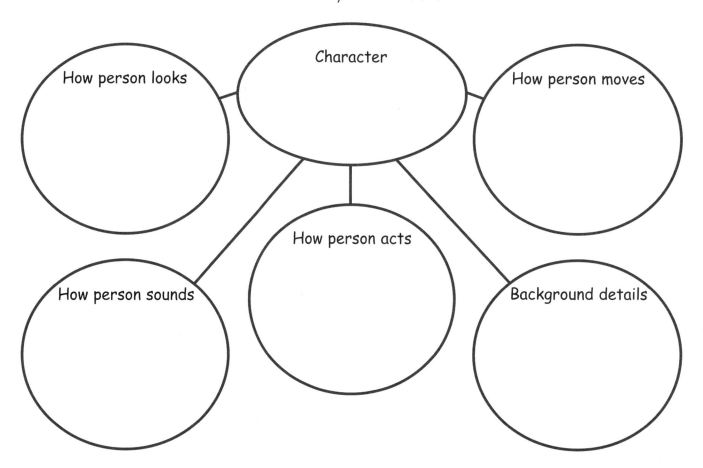

Lesson 8 The Writing Process: Descriptive Writing

As a final step in the prewriting stage, organize your ideas. How will you describe this person? Will you start with a physical description, perhaps from head to toe? Will you use order of importance to describe the overall person? Make a choice and write it here.

Method of organization: _____

Major details, in order:

Draft

Refer to your prewriting notes as you write a first draft. Remember, this is the time to get your ideas down on paper in sentences. This is not the time to worry about getting every word just right.

_____

_____

_____

_____

_____

_____

_____

_____

_____

_____

_____

Lesson 8 The Writing Process: Descriptive Writing

Revise

All writers face the difficult task of reading what they have just written and trying to make it better. Reread your draft carefully. Will the information be clear to your readers? Will it be interesting? Answer the questions below about your draft. If you answer "no" to any of the questions, then those are the areas that might need improvement.

- Did you keep your audience in mind? Did you include details that will interest them and that they will understand?

- Did you organize your description in a logical way?

- Did you use vivid verbs and precise nouns to help readers see the character?

- Did you use sensory details? To how many of your readers' senses did you appeal?

Rewrite your description here. Make changes to improve your writing, based on the questions you just answered.

_____

_____

_____

_____

_____

_____

_____

_____

_____

_____

_____

_____

_____

_____

_____

Lesson 8 | The Writing Process: Descriptive Writing

Proofread

Your description should be in good shape now. The last task is to check it for any remaining errors. It is best to check for one kind of error at a time. Proofread your revision on page 42. Use this checklist to help catch all of the errors.

_____ Does each sentence begin with a capital letter?

_____ Does each sentence have an appropriate end mark?

_____ Are proper nouns (names of people, places, or things) capitalized?

_____ Are all words spelled correctly?

When proofreaders work, they use certain symbols. Using these symbols makes their job easier. They will make your job easier, too.

Publish

Write a final copy of your description here. Use your best handwriting. Be careful not to introduce any new errors.

- Capitalize this letter.
- Add a missing end mark: . ? !
- Add a comma please.
- Fix incorrect or misspelled words.
- "Use quotation marks correctly," she reminded.
- Delete this word.
- Lowercase this letter.

Chapter 4
Lesson 1 Parts of a Fiction Story

A good story has these ingredients:

- A fiction story tells about made-up people or animals. They are the **characters** in the story.

- A fiction story has a **narrator**, or someone who tells the story The narrator might be a character in the story. Or the narrator might not take part in the action at all.

- A fiction story has a **setting** where the action takes place.

- A fiction story's action is the **plot**. The plot is usually a series of events that includes a **conflict**, which needs to be resolved.

- A fiction story uses **dialogue**, or conversation among characters, to move the action of the story along.

- **Sensory details** make the characters, setting, and action come alive.

- An interesting **beginning**, **middle**, and **end** make a fiction story fun to read.

Below is the first part of a fiction story. This story's narrator is one of the characters. In fact, he is the main character. Read the story, then answer the questions that follow.

My Normal Life

I'm not one of those kids you read about in books. I'm not rich, and I'm not poor. I'm just an average kid with an average family. Of course, it's not as if we sit around playing board games every night, either. They go to work; I go to school. We eat supper together most nights. Sometimes there are things to talk about. Sometimes there are not.

The only reason I've ever been out of Iowa is that I live by the Mississippi River. I can see Wisconsin across the river, and I've been to Wisconsin. So, by traveling a mile or two, I can say I have been out of state.

Dad is a mechanic. Mom says that's why our car is always breaking down. I guess it gives Dad extra practice. Mom is a cashier at Ivan's, the only grocery store in town. Dad says it's always good to know someone who can bring home the bacon without making an extra stop. That's a joke, I guess.

So, I'm a normal kid living in a normal town with parents about as normal as parents get. So, is this the beginning of the world's most boring story? It would be if I hadn't met Jeremiah.

Lesson 1 Parts of a Fiction Story

Jeremiah is not normal, like everyone else I know. Jeremiah says important things. But if he doesn't feel like it, he doesn't say anything at all. He's not rude, he just chooses what he wants to say and throws away what he doesn't want to say. That's one of the important things he said to me once.

Here's how I met Jeremiah. Mom sent me to Ivan's for eggs on her day off. It was a Wednesday, when the farmers set up stalls on the courthouse square. I dawdled next to the table full of homemade bread. Glory, it smelled good. Then, I wandered past the boxes of green beans and red radishes. Just looking at the onions made my eyes water. I tried to name the flowers in the galvanized pails. When I saw the eggs, though, I couldn't believe my eyes. They were brown! I looked around for a sign. I thought maybe they were a joke or something. No normal chicken would lay a brown egg, at least not that I ever saw at Ivan's. The man who was selling the eggs was watching me, and I was starting to feel a little...you know, watched.

"Nice eggs," I said. I figured that might lead to a clue about their origin. No. He just nodded. I had stood there too long not to buy something. I felt mild panic rising. I asked, "How much?"

The man's brown eyes slid over to a sign that I had completely missed. "Fresh Eggs $1.25," it said, in the neatest printing I had ever seen. I nodded, trying not to look as stupid as I felt.

"I'll take a dozen, please," I said, fishing in my pocket for the money Mom had given me. So, that's how I met Jeremiah. As you can tell, he threw away what he didn't want to say that day.

Lesson 1 Parts of a Fiction Story

Answer these questions about "My Normal Life." Look back at the story on pages 44 and 45 if you need to.

Who is the narrator?

_____

Who is the main character in the story?_____

List three details about the main character.

_____   _____   _____

In what way are details about the main character revealed?

_____

_____

What other characters appear in the story? What do you know about each character?

_____

_____

_____

Where does the action take place? _____

What kind of problem, or conflict, do you think might occur in this story? _____

_____

Review the brief dialogue. Notice what the characters say and how they say it. What do you learn about the characters from the dialogue?

Main character: _____

Other character: _____

Record some of the story's sensory details. Remember to look for sights, sounds, smells, textures, and tastes.

_____   _____   _____

_____   _____   _____

Lesson 2 Setting

The **setting** of a story is when and where the story's action takes place. The setting of a story may be in a real place or in a completely imagined place. The time during which a story takes place may be in the past, the present, or the future.

In some stories, the setting is very important. A mystery might depend completely on the creepy old house where the action takes place. In other stories, the characters' thoughts and actions are more important, and the setting is less vital.

Readers learn details of the setting in different ways. A character might say something about the weather or the scenery. Or, maybe you learn from a character's thoughts that he is annoyed by traffic noises, so you can assume he is in a big city. In other stories, the narrator describes the setting. Here is an example from "My Normal Life" on page 44.

> The only reason I've ever been out of Iowa is that I live by the Mississippi River. I can see Wisconsin across the river, and I've been to Wisconsin. So, by traveling a mile or two, I can say I have been out of state.
>
> Dad is a mechanic. Mom says that's why our car is always breaking down. I guess it gives Dad extra practice. Mom is a cashier at Ivan's, the only grocery store in town. Dad says it's always good to know someone who can bring home the bacon without making an extra stop. That's a joke, I guess.

What details does the narrator reveal about the setting?

_____   _____

_____   _____

_____   _____

Lesson 2 Setting

Here is another example. This passage is from "Song of the Trees," by Mildred D. Taylor. The narrator, who is also the main character, reveals details about the setting.

> I opened the window and looked outside. The earth was draped in a cloak of gray mist as the sun chased the night away. The cotton stalks, which in another hour would glisten greenly toward the sun, were gray. The ripening corn, wrapped in jackets of emerald and gold, was gray. Even the rich Mississippi earth was gray.
>
> Only the trees of the forest were not gray. They stood dark, almost black, across the dusty road, still holding the night. A soft breeze stirred, and their voices whispered down to me in a song of morning greeting.

What information do you get about the setting from this passage?

_____

_____

Write some of the sensory details Taylor used in the passage.

_____   _____

_____   _____

_____

What mood, or feeling, do you feel the details convey? Explain your answers.

_____

_____

Writers use details in their settings that match the mood of what is happening in the story. First, think about details that a writer might include in a story that is humorous or light-hearted.

What might the weather be like?

_____

_____

What time of day might it be?

_____

_____

Lesson 2 Setting

Now, think about setting details that a writer might include in a scary part of a story, or in a part where something bad is going to happen to a character.

What might the weather be like?

_____

_____

What time of day might it be?

_____

_____

List some words that would help reflect the mood of the scary part of the story.

_____   _____   _____

_____   _____   _____

Look over the details you recorded for "light-hearted" settings and "scary" or "bad" settings. Are you starting to imagine a great story? Choose one of the settings you have already begun to visualize and develop it further here.

Write a paragraph that describes the setting. Indicate both when and where the action takes place. Remember to organize your details in a way that makes sense. For example, if you are describing a distant view, you might go from left to right or from far to near. Think about which method makes most sense for your setting.

_____

_____

_____

_____

_____

_____

_____

_____

_____

_____

_____

Lesson 3 Characters

A good story has characters about whom readers care. Can you remember cheering for them when something good happened? Did you hope that the character's bad times would turn out all right? Name some characters you remember from stories or novels you have read.

_____   _____

_____   _____

Now, think about what you know about those characters. How did you learn about them? How did the narrator or author help you get to know the character? Normally, readers learn about characters in four ways:

- The narrator reveals information.

- The character's own words reveal information.

- The character's actions reveal information.

- Other characters' words and actions reveal information.

Review "My Normal Life," on pages 44 and 45. What do you know about the main character? For each detail you record, write how you know it. For example, in the second sentence you learn that the character is neither rich nor poor. You know this because the narrator (who is also the main character) reveals that information.

What I Know About the Character   How I Know It

_____   _____

_____   _____

_____   _____

_____   _____

_____   _____

_____   _____

_____   _____

_____   _____

_____   _____

_____   _____

_____   _____

Lesson 3 Characters

Now, think about a character you would like to create. Rather than thinking about what happens to the character, think about what kind of person the character is. Answer these questions.

Is the character human? _____ If not, what is the character? _____

Is the character male or female? _____

What two words best describe your character?

_____   _____

During what time period does your character live? _____

What background details or family history have "shaped" this character?

_____

What might your character say, and how? Write a line of dialogue that your character might speak.

_____

What might other characters say about this character? Either write a line of dialogue or describe what others would say.

_____

Now, introduce your character. Write a paragraph about him or her.

_____

_____

_____

_____

_____

_____

_____

_____

_____

_____

_____

_____

Lesson 4 Dialogue

Dialogue is the conversation among characters in a story. Good dialogue helps readers get to know the characters. Dialogue also moves the action of the story along.

"These aren't from Ivan's," Mom said as soon as she peeked into the egg carton to make sure I hadn't broken any. "Where did you get these?"

Uncertain about her reaction, I said as confidently as I could, "From the farm market. They're fresh."

She held one up. To my surprise, she didn't seem concerned about the color. Was I the only one who had never heard of brown eggs before? She asked, "Was it Mrs. Refsal's stall, then?"

I didn't think my mom paid any attention to the farm market. Now, all of a sudden, she knows these people by name? "Uhh, not unless Mrs. Refsal is a man."

She cocked her head and asked, "A man?"

"He was kinda tall. He had brown hair and brown eyes. He didn't say much." There, I had told her everything I knew.

"Oh," she nodded knowingly, "Jeremiah."

This is not normal. First, I discover brown eggs, about which my mom apparently knows everything. Now, she's on a first-name basis with people I have never even seen before.

What do you learn about the main character from this dialogue?

_____

What do you learn about the main character's mom?

_____

Take a closer look at a line of dialogue and its punctuation.

| The **tag line** tells who is speaking. | **Quotation marks** go before and after the speaker's exact words. |

She asked, "Was it Mrs. Refsal's stall, then?"

| A comma separates the tag line from the speaker's words. | End punctuation goes inside the quotation marks. |

The speaker's first word begins with a capital letter, even if that word is not the first word of the sentence.

Lesson 4 Dialogue

Below is some dialogue that has not been punctuated. Add the punctuation. Look at the dialogue on page 52 for examples if you need to. Pay close attention to the position of commas and end marks.

Who is Jeremiah I asked

She smiled suddenly and said I went to grade school with him

So, he's been around here all these years I quizzed.

Dialogue should sound like real people talking. A 12-year-old character should sound more or less like you sound. A grown-up should sound like a grown-up. Remember, however, that people sound different from each other. People have different speech patterns based on where they grew up and where they live.

Imagine you meet the main character of "My Normal Life" at the farm market. Write a conversation between yourself and that character. Remember, he lives in a small town in Iowa on the Mississippi River. See pages 44 and 45 to review other details. Think about what he might know that you don't know. What might you know that he doesn't? Make the dialogue sound realistic. Remember to use quotation marks and tag lines. If you wish, talk to the character about farm markets, brown eggs, or the Mississippi River.

_____

_____

_____

_____

_____

_____

_____

_____

_____

_____

_____

_____

_____

_____

_____

Lesson 5 Point of View

When a writer writes a story, he or she chooses a narrator to tell the story. In some stories, the narrator is one of the characters in the story. Words such as *I, me*, and *my* let readers know that a story is written from a **first-person point of view**. Here is another piece of "My Normal Life," the story begun on page 44.

> This is the first thing Jeremiah said to me. He said, "I have some green eggs, if you want 'em." I had been buying eggs from him every Wednesday most of the summer. In all those weeks, he hadn't said a word. I was thinking maybe he didn't speak. But then he came out with this green egg thing. Surely it was a joke. I stood there looking at his face. Of course, there was no sign whether it was a joke or whether he was just insane. I searched for a neutral answer.
>
> "I'll see if my mom wants some next week," was the best I could do. It got me off the hook, anyway. Maybe he'd think I was playing along, if it were a joke. Jeremiah just nodded.

Below is the same scene, but it is written in **third-person point of view**. Readers see words such as *he, she, him, her, his, they,* and *them* in stories that are written in third person. The main character is the same, but the narrator "reports" to readers what the character says, thinks, and does. A narrator who reveals characters' inner thoughts is said to be omniscient, or all-knowing.

> This is the first thing Jeremiah said to Max. He said, 'I have some green eggs, if you want 'em." Max had been buying eggs from Jeremiah every Wednesday most of the summer. In all those weeks, Jeremiah hadn't said a word. Max was thinking maybe this man didn't speak. But then Jeremiah came out with this green egg thing. Surely it was a joke. Max stood there looking at Jeremiah's face. Of course, there was no sign whether it was a joke or whether Jeremiah was just insane. Max searched for a neutral answer.
>
> "I'll see if my mom wants some next week," was the best Max could do. It got him off the hook, anyway. Maybe Jeremiah would think Max was playing along, if it was a joke. Jeremiah just nodded.

Lesson 5 Point of View

Look back at the piece of the story on page 54. How will Max ask his mother about the green eggs without embarrassing himself? Write the next conversation that Max has with his mom. Write in first-person, from Max's point of view. Remember to punctuate your dialogue correctly.

_____

_____

_____

_____

_____

_____

_____

_____

_____

Now, write that same scene in third-person point of view. Remember, the main character, Max, is the same. However, your omniscient narrator will tell what he says, thinks, and does.

_____

_____

_____

_____

_____

_____

_____

_____

_____

_____

Lesson 6 Story Ideas

Many stories, such as "My Normal Life," are **realistic**. They include human characters who are more or less regular people. Realistic stories set in the past are called historical fiction. Whether the setting is in the past or the present, though, the characters could be real, and the events could happen, even though the details come from a writer's imagination.

List some stories or books you have read that have realistic settings.

_____   _____

_____   _____

What kind of realistic story would you like to write? Will it be about a regular kid who loves to ride his bike? Might it be about the first person in your town to own an automobile? Realistic stories require just as much imagination as unrealistic, or fantasy, stories do. Write down some realistic story ideas.

Realistic story idea #1

Character(s): _____

Setting:_____

Plot:_____

_____

Realistic story idea #2

Character(s): _____

Setting:_____

Plot:_____

_____

Realistic story idea #3

Character(s): _____

Setting:_____

Plot:_____

_____

Lesson 6 Story Ideas

There are different types of fiction that are not realistic, such as fantasy, tall tales, and science fiction. A **fantasy's** setting may be anywhere and at any time. Characters may be human or some other life form. Details often involve characters with special powers who go on amazing and dangerous quests, and who are victorious over a "bad" or evil force or enemy.

What fantasies have you read? Try to recall some of the details. Were there talking animals? Where did the characters live? Did the author specify a time period? Record a few details that you remember.

_____

_____

What kind of fantasy would you like to write? Who will be your main characters? What kind of life form are they? Where will they live? Why are they there? What is the time period? Open up your imagination and jot down a couple of fantasy ideas here.

Fantasy idea #1

Character(s): _____

Setting: _____

Plot: _____

_____

Fantasy idea #2

Character(s): _____

Setting: _____

Plot: _____

_____

Fantasy idea #3

Character(s): _____

Setting: _____

Plot: _____

_____

Lesson 7 The Writing Process: Story

Some writers base their settings on their own experiences. Perhaps a character's school is similar to a school the author used to attend. Maybe a character's teacher is much like a teacher the author once had. Other writers create whole new worlds, maybe even places where human beings don't exist. Use the writing process and see what kind of world you can create.

Prewrite

Look at the story ideas you wrote on pages 56 and 57. Choose one of those ideas, or another idea that you like, and begin to develop it. Whether you write a realistic story or fantasy, you need to pay special attention to your main character. Use this idea web to record details about how he or she looks, acts, speaks, and so on.

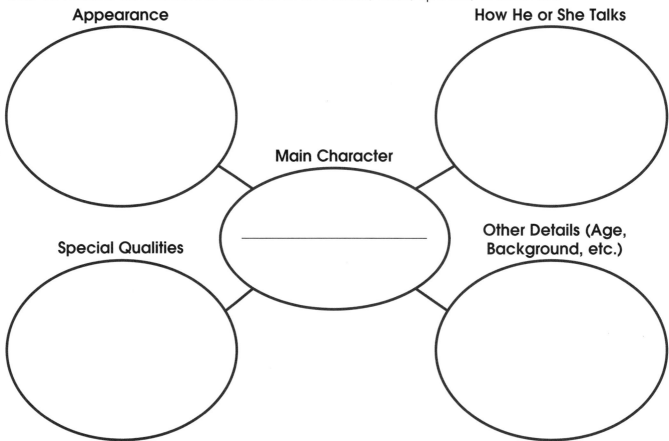

Appearance

How He or She Talks

Main Character

_____

Special Qualities

Other Details (Age, Background, etc.)

Before you go on, consider these questions about your setting and plot.

—What is the setting of your story? Consider place or location, time setting (year), season, time of day, and weather.

—What problem will the main character face?

—What does the character do to try to solve the problem? Does it take more than one try? What is the final solution or outcome?

Lesson 7 The Writing Process: Story

Now, put the main events of your story together. Think about the story you are about to tell. What is at the beginning, in the middle, and at the end? Use the story map on this page to plan the important parts of your story.

Character(s)

_____

Setting

_____

Plot: Beginning

_____

_____

_____

_____

Plot: Middle

_____

_____

_____

_____

_____

_____

_____

Plot: End

_____

_____

_____

_____

Lesson 7 The Writing Process: Story

Draft

Write a first draft. Refer to your story map as you work. Continue on another sheet of paper if you need to. As you write, don't worry about mistakes. Just get your ideas down in sentences and in order.

_____

_____

_____

_____

_____

_____

_____

_____

_____

_____

_____

_____

_____

_____

_____

_____

_____

_____

_____

_____

_____

_____

Write an idea for a title here. You may choose the final title later.

Title:_____

Lesson 7 The Writing Process: Story

Revise

Revising your own writing is a difficult job. It's hard, even for an experienced writer, to change or "fix" something that you worked hard to write.

Answer the questions below. If you answer "no" to any of these questions, those are the areas you might need to improve. Make marks on your draft so you know what needs attention.

- Did you give details about an interesting character and a setting?
- Does your story have a beginning, a middle, and an end?
- Did you include a problem and a solution in your plot?
- Did you tell events in an order that made sense?
- Did you use sensory details?
- Did you use dialogue to help readers learn about characters and to move the story forward?

Review the important parts of a story.

- In the **beginning** of a story, readers meet the character or characters and learn a little about the setting and the plot. The first sentence makes readers want to keep on reading.

- In the **middle** of a story, the action takes place. Readers see the character or characters face a problem. The characters probably make one or more attempts to solve the problem.

- In the **end**, the characters solve the problem in a logical way. Keep in mind that it is not satisfying to have a story's central problem just go away by magic or by coincidence. Your characters must deal with their problem to solve it.

On your draft, draw brackets next to the beginning, middle, and end of your story. Jot some notes if you decide that you must revise any of those parts to make them more interesting for your readers.

Lesson 7 The Writing Process: Story

Read your draft out loud. Listen for awkward sentences or sentences that sound too much the same. Then, write the revision of your story here. Fix any awkward sentences as you go.

_____

_____

_____

_____

_____

_____

_____

_____

_____

_____

_____

_____

_____

_____

_____

_____

_____

_____

_____

_____

_____

_____

_____

_____

Review your title choices. Which one seems best? Write it here.

Title:_____

Lesson 7 The Writing Process: Story

Proofread

By now you have read your story several times through. You can probably recite parts from memory. It is still important, though, to proofread carefully. When you are familiar with what you are reading, you are more likely to overlook errors. Also, you must still proofread typewritten text, even if the computer has checked your spelling. If you type *threw* instead of *throw*, for example, the computer won't catch that error. Use the checklist below as you proofread your revised story. Look for one kind of error at a time.

____ Each sentence begins with a capital letter.

____ Each sentence ends with the correct punctuation (period, question mark, or exclamation point).

____ Dialogue is punctuated correctly.

____ Each sentence states a complete thought.

____ All words are spelled correctly.

When proofreaders work, they use certain symbols. Using these symbols will make your job easier as you proofread your story. Remember to read your writing out loud. When you read out loud, you may hear mistakes or rough spots that you did not see.

- <u>c</u>apitalize this letter.
- Add a missing end mark: ⊙ ? !
- Add a comma please.
- "Be sure to punctuate your dialogue," she said.
- Fix incorrect or misspelled words.
- ~~Delete~~ this word.
- Lowercase this Letter.

Publish

Write a final copy of your story on a separate sheet of paper. Write or type carefully so that there are no mistakes. If you wish, add illustrations and make a neat cover or title page. Share your story with friends and family.

Chapter 5

Lesson 1 Persuasive Writing

In persuasive writing, a writer tries to make readers think, feel, or act in a certain way. You may not be aware of it, but you see persuasive writing every day. Park benches and buses carry signs for restaurants, TV stations, and grocery stores. In your favorite magazine, you read the letters to the editor. In the school newspaper, a fellow student has written an article about the library. Here is an example of a persuasive article. The writer gives some information and states his opinion. He closes with a statement that invites his readers to take action.

A Message to Readers

By Daniel Murphy

Our school should rethink the library and its use. Any teacher will tell you how important reading is. And reading, of course, involves having access to books. The students at WRMS don't have that access. The library is not open before or after school, and there is not enough time between classes.

I think we could make some small adjustments to the daily schedule and create a 20-minute reading period at the start of each day. Students would be responsible for having a book to read. And each student could have one library pass a week to use during the 20-minute period.

By choosing their own reading material, students are more likely to be motivated to read on their own. By making time for reading, the school sends the message that reading and books are important. I think that would be an excellent message for this school to send to students, parents, and the community.

Lesson 1 Persuasive Writing

Do you think it would be important to have a reading period in middle school? Do you think a special reading time is not necessary? Respond to Daniel's article on page 64. State your opinion and support it with reasons. Assume that your article will appear in the school newspaper. Make sure that your opinion is clear, and that readers understand what you want them to think or do. How persuasive can you be?

_____

_____

_____

_____

_____

_____

_____

_____

_____

_____

_____

_____

_____

_____

_____

_____

_____

_____

_____

_____

_____

_____

_____

_____

_____

Lesson 2 Facts and Opinions

Which of these sentences is a fact? Which is an opinion? If you're not sure, ask yourself these questions: Which statement could be proven true? That would be a **fact**. Which is a belief or a personal judgment? That would be an **opinion**.

Every middle school in the state has a library.

Libraries are the best sources for books and information.

Often, writers state both facts and opinions. That is okay, but both writers and readers must be able to tell the difference between the two. Also, even opinions should be backed up with facts. Look for facts and opinions as you re-read Daniel's article.

A Message to Readers

By Daniel Murphy

Our school should rethink the library and its use. Any teacher will tell you how important reading is. And reading, of course, involves having access to books. The students at WRMS don't have that access. The library is not open before or after school, and there is not enough time between classes.

I think we could make some small adjustments to the daily schedule and create a 20-minute reading period at the start of each day. Students would be responsible for having a book to read. And each student could have one library pass a week to use during the 20-minute period.

By choosing their own reading material, students are more likely to be motivated to read on their own. By making time for reading, the school sends the message that reading and books are important. I think that would be an excellent message for this school to send to students, parents, and the community.

Lesson 2 Facts and Opinions

Words such as *think*, *believe*, *should*, *must*, *never*, *always*, *like*, *hate*, *best*, and *worst* may signal that a statement is an opinion. Read the article again and circle any opinion words you find.

Write two facts from the article.

_____

_____

Write two opinions from the article.

_____

_____

One of Daniel's classmates has written her own opinion about the issue of reading and the school library. Read Juanita's paragraph. Watch for opinion signal words.

> I think that we should take Daniel Murphy's idea even further. I know so many kids who don't really know what's in the library. They don't know how to find information when they have to do a school report. This school should offer a class on how to do research. There is so much information out there. We need to learn how to find it and use it.

Write one fact from Juanita's paragraph.

_____

Circle any opinion words that you find in Juanita's paragraph. Then, write one opinion that Juanita states.

_____

Now, state your own opinion about the library at your school. Is it well used or could access to it be improved?

_____

_____

Lesson 3 Emotional Appeals

How do persuasive writers get readers to think, feel, or act in a certain way? Often, they appeal to readers' emotions. When writers make an emotional appeal, they try to get at something about which readers feel strongly. For example, Mrs. Quinlan, the school librarian, thinks the library is being neglected. She included this statement in a letter to the editor.

> If the school board wants a "better" library, they're going to have to pay for it. I try to maintain up-to-date equipment and resources for our students and teachers. I am doing so with the smallest budget I've had in my 20 years as a librarian. How a school system spends its money sends a message to the community. What is important to us?

Mrs. Quinlan knows that most people feel strongly about education and about their local schools and how tax dollars are spent. Though her statements are mostly opinions, rather than facts, they have a strong emotional appeal and may persuade some readers to believe as she does.

Many people have strong feelings about issues such as these:

justice	family	safety	education
money	home	security	conservation
injustice	crime	waste	violence

Think about what "makes you mad" or what makes you feel really good when you listen to the news or read newspaper or magazine articles. Name some issues about which you have strong feelings.

_____ _____ _____

_____ _____ _____

Lesson 3 Emotional Appeals

Dear Editor:

I have two kids in school, and I occasionally volunteer at the middle school. While there recently, I worked in a room across the hall from the library. The library looked like a dark cave. During the whole morning, I saw only two students go into the library.

At lunchtime, I wandered in. I saw a lone librarian sitting at the main desk, and one student working on the computer in the corner. The librarian was reviewing book catalogs but said she had no budget to acquire new books for the rest of this school year. When I asked why it was so dark, she said that there were electrical problems, but the school had put off fixing the area because it was "nonessential."

I am outraged. How can our children learn if they don't have a library? How can they prepare for high school if they don't learn how to do research? The school system is sending the message that books are not important. Is that the message we really want to send?

T. Tavenor

Read the letter to the editor at left. What kind of emotional appeal does the writer make? Explain the emotional appeal in T. Tavenor's letter to the editor.

_____

_____

_____

_____

Write a letter to the editor in response to T. Tavenor's letter. Write in support of her opinion, or indicate why you disagree with her, and tell why. Remember to consider your audience. What kind of emotional appeal might make people agree with you?

Dear Editor:

_____

_____

_____

_____

_____

_____

_____

_____

_____

_____

_____

_____

_____

_____

_____

Lesson 4 Advertising

Advertising copywriters rely heavily on emotional appeals to win over, or persuade, consumers. Advertisers know that people have strong feelings about wanting to feel good, to fit in, and to have fun. Advertisements constantly send messages that writers think people want to hear.

Look at the Grandma Renata's logo. Why does the ad include the phrase "Your Family Restaurant"?

_____

_____

What message does the Cheer! slogan send?

_____

_____

For advertising copywriters, thinking about audience is especially important. Perhaps the most often-asked questions are these: Who might buy this product? What kind of message can persuade them to buy?

Imagine you are writing an advertisement for a new action movie that is coming out this summer. Who is your audience?

_____

To what strong feelings do you need to appeal to get this audience to see your movie?

_____

Lesson 4 Advertising

You are an advertising copywriter. Think up a slogan for a new music group. First, think about who the audience is. About what kinds of issues might they have strong feelings? In your slogan, make an emotional appeal.

Your next assignment is to create a slogan for a new mall. Remember your audience and make an emotional appeal.

Finally, make up a slogan for your state. (If your state already has a slogan, make up a new one.) The slogan should make residents feel proud of their state and should make other people want to visit.

Images can make emotional appeals, as well, and most advertisements use a combination of words and images to persuade you to buy a product. Look back at the slogans you created. Choose your favorite and create an image to accompany it. Your slogan and image should work together to make a strong emotional appeal. Create your ad in this space.

Lesson 5 Order of Importance

When you write about events, you use time order. When you describe a place, you use spatial order. When you write to persuade, you should use **order of importance.**

Remember, when writers write to persuade, they try to make their readers think or act in a certain way. As you persuade, save your most important ideas—your strongest arguments—for last. Build ideas from least important to most important.

Here is part of a letter that Meng wrote to his principal. Notice the reasons he gives for getting involved with the charity project.

To prepare children for reading, the Literacy Board will distribute books to youngsters as young as 1 year old. The Literacy Board is a non-profit organization and needs our help for this important project. For every dollar our school contributes to "Ready to Read," the Board will distribute four books. Providing books to families with young children will encourage parents to read with their children. Children who are read to at home are far more likely to be ready to read when they enter kindergarten. Studies show that students who enter school ready to read are likely to have more successful school careers than students who are not "reading ready" upon kindergarten entry.

Meng gave several reasons for why students at his school should contribute to this particular project. Number them in the paragraph. Then, underline the most important reason.

Lesson 5 Order of Importance

What project should your school raise money for? Think of a worthy cause. Then, write a letter to your teacher or principal. Try to persuade the person that your idea is a good one. Ask yourself this: What will make this person want to support my idea?

Before you begin drafting your letter, write your reasons here. Then, number them in the order in which you will use them in your letter. Save the strongest argument, or the most important reason, for last.

Reason: _____

Reason: _____

Reason: _____

Reason: _____

Dear _____,

Lesson 6 Letter of Complaint

A business letter is a letter written to a company, organization, or person you do not know. In a letter of complaint, the writer usually expresses a complaint, then asks the recipient to do something. It is important to be very clear about the action the recipient should take. Read this letter of complaint. Notice its six parts.

The **heading** includes the sender's address and the date.	2763 Turner Street Randolph, WI 53956 February 19, 2008
The **inside address** is the name and address of the recipient.	Falcon Electronics 731 Industry Way Greenwood, SC 29647
A colon follows the **greeting**.	Dear Falcon Electronics:
The text of the letter is the **body**.	I am returning the Falcon CD changer, Model 67F, that I purchased one month ago. The unit is not functioning correctly. When multiple CDs are loaded, the "Random Play" function does not work. According to your product guarantee, I have the right to choose whether you repair or replace this unit. I would prefer that you replace this unit with the same or a similar model.
A comma follows the **closing**.	Cordially,
The sender always includes a **signature**.	*Terri Jansen* Terri Jansen

Lesson 6 Letter of Complaint

Imagine you recently purchased something that doesn't work right or is flawed in some way. Write a letter of complaint to the company. Be sure to make a reasonable, clear request at the end so the recipient knows what action you expect. Remember to include the six parts of a business letter.

Lesson 7 The Writing Process: Persuasive Article

What would you like to change about your school? Your neighborhood? Your town? Can you persuade others to agree with you? Use the writing process to plan and write a persuasive article.

Prewrite

Think of issues about which you feel strongly. What would you like to change? How would you like to change it? Make notes here about some things you would like to change.

_____   _____

_____   _____

_____   _____

Now, think about these issues for a few minutes. About which one do you feel most strongly? Choose the issue you will write about.

_____

Use this idea web to collect your reasons for seeking change. Think about why you are unsatisfied. You may state opinions, but you must also give reasons or facts. Also, consider what action you expect readers to take. Add more ovals to the idea web if you need to.

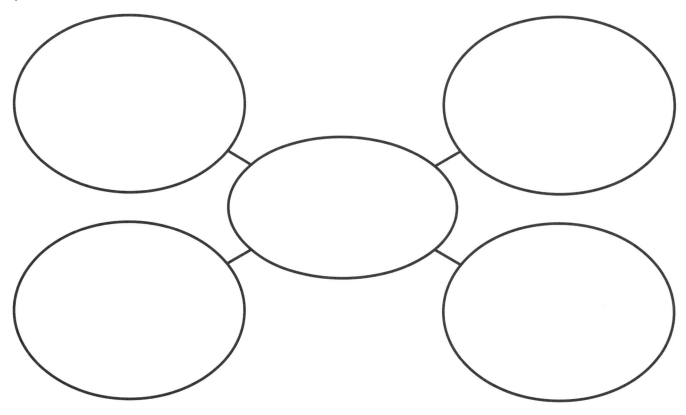

Lesson 7 The Writing Process: Persuasive Article

Now, it is time to organize the points you will make in your persuasive article. What is your strongest argument? Save that one for last. Write your important reasons or points in order in these boxes.

[ ]

[ ]

[ ]

[ ]

[ ]

Lesson 7 The Writing Process: Persuasive Article

Draft

Write a first draft of your article on this page. Refer to your chart on page 77. As you write, don't worry about spelling or punctuation. Just get your ideas down in sentences and in order.

_____

_____

_____

_____

_____

_____

_____

_____

_____

_____

_____

_____

_____

_____

_____

_____

_____

_____

_____

_____

_____

_____

_____

_____

_____

Lesson 7 The Writing Process: Persuasive Article

Revise

Even the most experienced writers look over their work and make changes. Reread your own work slowly and carefully. Then, answer the questions below about your draft. If you answer "no" to any of these questions, those are the areas that might need improvement. Feel free to make marks on your draft, so you know what needs more work.

> • Did you state your opinion clearly?
>
> • Did you give strong reasons to support your opinion?
>
> • Did you organize those reasons in a logical order, such as least important to most important?
>
> • Did you clearly state what you want readers to think or do?

With persuasive writing, it is especially important to aim your arguments right at your specific audience. Ask yourself these questions.

• What opinions does my audience already hold about this issue?

• What does my audience already know about this issue?

• What will they need to know in order to understand the issue?

• What emotional appeals might sway the audience in my direction? Will certain words affect the appeal?

As you revise, read your work out loud. Hearing the words might allow you to catch awkward sentences or ideas that don't flow smoothly.

Lesson 7 The Writing Process: Persuasive Article

Write your revised article here. As you revise, remember to keep your audience in mind.

_____

_____

_____

_____

_____

_____

_____

_____

_____

_____

_____

_____

_____

_____

_____

_____

_____

_____

_____

_____

_____

_____

_____

_____

_____

_____

Lesson 7 The Writing Process: Persuasive Article

Proofread

Now is the time to correct those last little mistakes. You will be a better proofreader if you look for just one kind of error at a time. So, look for capital letters first, then look for end punctuation, then for spelling, and so on. Here is a checklist to use as you proofread your revised article.

_____ Each sentence begins with a capital letter.

_____ Each sentence ends with the correct punctuation (period, question mark, or exclamation point).

_____ Each sentence states a complete thought.

_____ All words are spelled correctly. (If you're not sure, check a dictionary.)

Use these symbols as you proofread your article. Remember to read your writing out loud, just as you did at the revising stage. You may hear mistakes or rough spots that you did not catch when you reread your work.

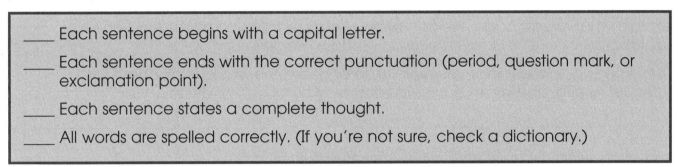

- Capitalize this letter.
- Write in a missing end mark like this: ⊙ ? !
- Insert a comma please.
- Fix incorrect or misspelled word like this.
- Delete this word.
- Lowercase this letter.

Publish

Write or type a final copy of your article on a separate sheet of paper. Work carefully and neatly so that there are no mistakes.

Lesson 1 Explanatory Writing

Some explanatory writing is simple. A sign says "In," and you know where to enter a building. Some explanations are not simple. A new cell phone might come with a whole book full of instructions. Your new bicycle could come in a small box, with instructions to assemble the dozens of parts, one by one.

Some explanatory writing does not take the form of instructions, though. Some explanations tell how or why something happened. For example, your teacher might explain what events cause the formation of a desert. Or you might read an explanation of why your favorite music group is breaking up.

List some explanations that you have read or heard this week. Think about your science, health, and social studies classes, play practices, or athletic team practices.

_____   _____

_____   _____

_____   _____

_____   _____

Think about instructions you have read or used. How many different kinds can you list?

_____ _____ _____ _____

_____ _____ _____ _____

When you write to explain, or give instructions, you might write for these reasons:

- to tell how to make something
- to tell how something works
- to tell how to get somewhere
- to tell why something happened

Lesson 1 Explanatory Writing

Here is a simple explanation that tells how to plant a bean seed.

   First, prepare the soil by loosening it with a trowel. Then, place the seed on the soil. Cover the seed with half an inch of soil and lightly tamp it down. Finally, water the ground thoroughly.

The writer stated each step in order. To help readers follow the steps, she used order words such as *first*, *then*, and *finally* to make the order clear. Underline each of those order words that you find in the paragraph above.

What do you know how to do? Write down a few simple processes, such as making toast, that you think you could explain clearly.

_____   _____

_____   _____

Now, choose one of the processes you listed and think carefully about each of its steps. Imagine that you are explaining the process to someone who has never done it before. You will have to start at the very beginning. List the steps here.

Process: _____

Step 1: _____

Step 2: _____

Step 3: _____

Step 4: _____

Step 5: _____

Step 6: _____

Step 7: _____

Step 8: _____

Step 9: _____

Step 10: _____

Step 11: _____

Step 12: _____

Step 13: _____

Step 14: _____

Step 15: _____

Lesson 2 Cause-and-Effect Relationships

Why is milk "milky?" Why does a cactus have spines? When you ask why, you are looking for causes. A **cause** is a reason why something happens. An **effect** is a thing that happens. Here are some examples of causes and effects. Think about the relationship between each cause and effect.

Cause	Effect
It is cold outside.	Hugh wore a coat.
I lost my house key.	I called Mom at work.
Lou's car won't start.	She rode the bus home.

When writers write to explain, they often use causes and effects. They use the words and phrases *so, because, as a result*, and *therefore* to link causes and effects. Read this paragraph about why the fish population is changing. Circle the cause-and-effect words and phrases in the paragraph.

The fish populations in the Green River are returning to normal levels. Four years ago, there was an oil tanker spill at Branton Manufacturing in Parnett. As a result, nearly 20 miles of the Green River were polluted. The oil slick choked out vegetation, so all species of fish and amphibians lost their food supply and died. Now, the river is nearly healthy again because of the diligent clean-up work carried out by so many concerned citizens.

Find some causes and effects in the previous paragraph. One is written for you. Write two other causes and effects.

Cause	Effect
There was an oil spill.	Twenty miles of river were polluted.

Lesson 2 Cause-and-Effect Relationships

Writers might also use causes and effects when they tell about events that happened in a story or novel. Here are some causes and effects from *The Thief Lord* by Cornelia Funke.

Prosper and Bo's parents are dead, and they must live with an aunt and uncle who treat them cruelly. The brothers run away to Venice. Once there, they meet an unusual boy who calls himself the "Thief Lord." The Thief Lord offers the boys food and shelter along with several other children. Though the boys are grateful, they soon get caught up in petty crime, and a mysterious turn of events puts all the children in danger.

Find the causes and effects in the paragraph above. Write them here. The first one is done for you.

Cause	Effect
The boys' parents are dead.	The boys live with an aunt and uncle.

Think about a story or novel you have read recently. What happened, and what did the characters do? Think about the events in terms of causes and effects. Ask yourself questions such as these: What caused this event to happen? What effect did this event have?

Write the causes and effects of some important events from the book.

Book title: _____

_____

_____

_____

_____

_____

_____

_____

_____

_____

Lesson 3 Report an Event

In a news report, a reporter writes about an event. The event might be a fire, a governor's press conference, or a hurricane. In addition to relating events in the order in which they occurred, the reporter links causes and effects. Causes and effects help readers understand what happens and why.

Here is part of a report about a house fire. Look for words that signal cause-and-effect relationships: *so, because, as a result, therefore*. When you find them, circle them.

Write three causes and three effects from the paragraph.

> The Ford Township Fire Department made a run on Monday afternoon as the result of a 911 call at 2:45 p.m. The caller, a homeowner on Murphy Road, reported seeing heavy smoke at a garage belonging to his neighbor, Abe Samson. When the trucks arrived at the scene, the structure was engulfed in smoke. Because of the caller's quick action, firefighters were able to save the structure. Samson was not home at the time. Firefighters discovered an electric heater with frayed wiring, so Chief Will Layman suspected an electrical spark from faulty wiring as the cause of the fire.

Cause: _____   Effect:_____

_____   _____

Cause: _____   Effect:_____

_____   _____

Cause: _____   Effect:_____

_____   _____

Lesson 3 Report an Event

Now, think about causes and effects in an event in your own life. What happened on the way to school yesterday? At lunch? After your parents got home from work? Even if nothing "big" or exciting happened, there were causes and effects in action. What did you do? What happened next? What resulted from these happenings? List some events in order. Draw arrows to show any cause-and-effect relationship among events.

1. _____

2. _____

3. _____

4. _____

5. _____

Now, practice writing about causes and effects. Write a paragraph about the happenings you listed above. Remember to use *so, because, as a result,* and *therefore* to connect the cause-and-effect relationships.

_____

_____

_____

_____

_____

_____

_____

_____

_____

_____

_____

_____

_____

_____

_____

_____

_____

Lesson 4 Graphics and Visual Aids

What is a picture worth? If you're putting together a piece of furniture, a picture to go along with the instructions can make the difference between success and failure. Sometimes, words can only do so much. Then, you need a picture to help out. "Pictures" may take the form of drawings, photographs, maps, graphs, or diagrams.

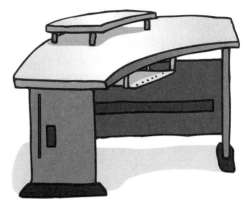

Imagine writing out a bus schedule in paragraph form. Would you rather get your information from the paragraph on the left or the table on the right?

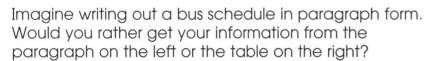

Bus 16A departs the depot at 6:24 a.m. Its first stop is at 6:28 a.m. at Bus Stop 21, at the corner of Lincoln Ave. and 4th St. Its second stop is at 6:31 a.m. at Bus Stop 27, in front of 347 Morgan Ave. Its third stop is at 6:37 a.m. at Bus stop 40, in the outlot at the Central Plaza Shopping Center.

Bus 16A		
Place	**Destination**	**Time**
Departure		6:24 a.m.
BS 21	Lincoln Av/4th	6:28 a.m.
BS 27	347 Morgan Av	6:31 a.m.
BS 40	Ctrl. Pl. Sh. Ctr.	6:37 a.m.

At each bus stop, a schedule indicates which buses stop there, at what time, and where the buses go. Use the information in the paragraph, below, to create a table that shows the schedule posted at Bus Stop 40.

At 6:37 a.m., Bus 16A stops, destined for Clayton College. At 6:48 a.m., Bus 2A stops, destined for all points north. At 7:01 a.m., Bus 44D stops, destined for College Mall. At 7:12 a.m., Bus 24C stops, destined for downtown. At 7:28 a.m., Bus 7A stops, destined for Clayton College.

Bus Stop 40		
Time	**Bus #**	**Destination**

Lesson 4 Graphics and Visual Aids

A table is just one way to show information in a visual way. Diagrams, bar graphs, circle graphs, and pictographs are also good tools. Here is a bar graph that shows how the number of bus riders on Bus 16A has changed during the last ten years.

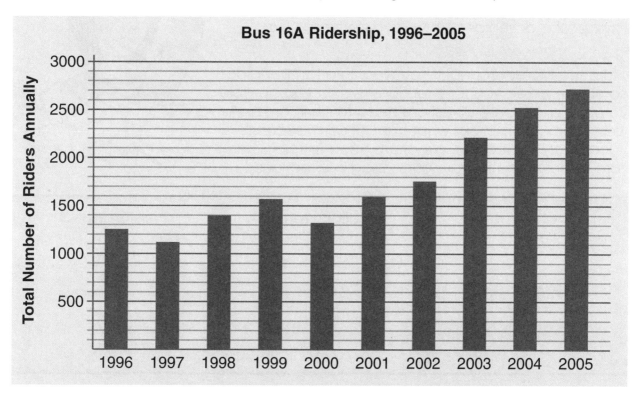

Now, create your own visual aid. Imagine that you are keeping track of the total number of students in your school. Perhaps you want to show how much each student in your class has contributed to a school fundraiser. Think about how you could show the information in a creative and meaningful way with a table or graph. Acquire or make up data, if necessary, and write it in the space below. Then, add your visual aid.

Data

Lesson 5 Directions

Imagine you are in a place where you have never been before. Someone has told you to go to the second hallway, turn left, turn left again, and the place you are looking for will be "right there." But, you have been down three hallways, past a dozen doorways, and nothing makes sense.

Now, turn the tables around. If you were in a familiar place and someone asked you for directions, would you be able to give clear directions? Directions need to be in order. As you write them, think about what happens first, second, next, and so on. In addition, directions need to tell "where." Here are some words that are often used in directions.

Time-Order Words	Direction Words	Position Words
first	left	over
second	right	under
then	up	past
next	down	beyond
after that	north	before
finally	west	above
		beside

Here is how Cassie told her friend Hanna how to get to the new store at College Mall. Underline the time-order, direction, and position words in the paragraph.

> First, enter the mall at the west entrance off of Autumn Road. Walk past the information center and go down the mallway to the right. Then, when you get to the "T," go right again. After that turn, go up the stairs. Tammy's is just beyond the bookstore.

Lesson 5 Directions

Write directions that tell how to get from one place to another in your school or in another large place with which you are familiar. If you need to, close your eyes and imagine yourself walking from one place to the other. Now, write your directions. If you need to, look back to page 90 for time-order, direction, and position words.

_____

_____

_____

_____

_____

_____

_____

_____

Imagine that you live in a tree house at the center of a tropical island. Friends have arrived at the beach, and they need to know how to get to your tree house. Write directions so they can find the way. If you wish, make a sketch of the island on a separate sheet of paper. Then, write the directions here.

_____

_____

_____

_____

_____

_____

_____

_____

_____

_____

Lesson 6 The Writing Process: How-to Instructions

Someone has asked you to explain how to play a popular card game. Can you do it? Use the writing process to see how good you are at explaining to someone else how to do something.

Prewrite

Think about things that you know how to do. You might think about that card game, about a computer program, or about your favorite food. Write down some things that you know how to do or make.

_____   _____

_____   _____

_____   _____

Look over your list and imagine explaining how to do each thing. With which topic are you most comfortable? Explore the idea by writing down everything you can think of about that topic. Add to this idea web as you need to.

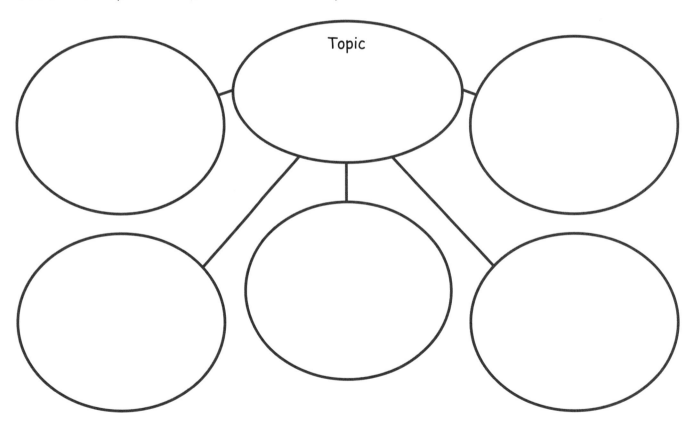

Are you comfortable with your topic? If not, go back to your list and choose another. Explore it with an idea web on a separate sheet of paper. Remember to think about your audience. What will they need to know?

Lesson 6 The Writing Process: How-to Instructions

Now, it is time to put the steps in order. Think about the process you are about to explain. Assume that your audience has never done this before, so you need to start at the very beginning. Use the sequence chart on this page to list the important steps in your explanation. Don't worry about details here; just be sure to list the main steps in the correct order.

1. _____

2. _____

3. _____

4. _____

5. _____

6. _____

7. _____

8. _____

9. _____

Lesson 6 The Writing Process: How-to Instructions

Draft

In the space below, write a first draft of your instructions. Keep your sequence chart on hand as you write. Continue on another sheet of paper if you need to. As you write, don't worry about getting everything perfect. Just get your ideas down in sentences and paragraphs and in order.

_____

_____

_____

_____

_____

_____

_____

_____

_____

_____

_____

_____

_____

_____

_____

_____

_____

_____

_____

_____

_____

_____

_____

_____

_____

Lesson 6 The Writing Process: How-to Instructions

Revise

For many writers, revising is much more difficult than writing the first draft. Try to reread your work with fresh eyes. Answer the questions below about your draft. If you answer "no" to any questions, those are the areas that might need improvement. Make marks on your draft, so you know what needs more work.

- Did you explain how to do something from beginning to end?

- Did you include all of the steps in order?

- Did you include time-order words to make the sequence clear?

- Did you use direction and position words to make your details clear?

- Did you use good describing words so your readers can "see" what they are supposed to do?

- Did you keep your audience in mind by asking yourself what they might already know or what they need to know?

- Did you include a heading or title so readers know what they are reading about?

Recognizing causes and effects helps readers understand what they are reading. The words *so, because, therefore,* and *as a result* may signal a cause-effect relationship. Here is an example:

> Shape the cookies into balls. Make them all the same size so that they bake evenly. Leave at least two inches between each cookie because the cookies will spread as they bake. After removing cookies from the oven, remove from cookie sheet immediately. Leaving them on the sheet would result in brown, over-baked bottoms.

Look back at your draft and think about cause-and-effect relationships. Are the causes and effects clear? Do you need to add signal words to make them more clear?

Lesson 6 The Writing Process: How-to Instructions

Write the revision of your instructions here. As you revise, remember to think about important details that your readers will need to know.

_____

_____

_____

_____

_____

_____

_____

_____

_____

_____

_____

_____

_____

_____

_____

_____

_____

_____

_____

_____

_____

_____

_____

_____

_____

_____

_____

_____

_____

_____

Lesson 6 The Writing Process: How-to Instructions

Proofread

Now it is time to correct any last little mistakes. Good proofreaders look for just one kind of error at a time. So, read through once for capital letters. Read again for end punctuation, spelling, and so on. Here is a checklist to use as you proofread your instructions.

> ____ Each sentence begins with a capital letter.
>
> ____ Each sentence ends with the correct punctuation (period, question mark, or exclamation point).
>
> ____ Each sentence states a complete thought.
>
> ____ All words are spelled correctly.

Use standard proofreading symbols as you proofread your own revised instructions.

As you proofread, remember to read your writing out loud, even if there is no one to listen. When you read, you may hear mistakes or awkward spots that you did not see.

- Capitalize this letter.
- Add a missing end mark: . ? !
- Insert a comma please.
- Fix incorect or misspelled words.
- Delete this word.
- Lowercase this letter.

Publish

Write a final copy of your instructions on a separate sheet of paper. Write or type carefully and neatly so that there are no mistakes. If you wish, include a graph, chart, or diagram to enhance your instructions and to make them more clear. Read your instructions out loud or perform a demonstration in front of an audience.

Chapter 7
Lesson 1 Informational Writing

When writers write to inform, they present information about a topic. You do this when you write reports for school. Here is a report that Benito wrote about Ecuador.

Ecuador

In Ecuador, the South American republic named after the equator, one might expect sweltering heat. But visitors and residents know otherwise. The republic's topography, or land features, create a varied climate that suits a number of lifestyles.

The hot climate expected of equatorial regions occurs in two sections of Ecuador. Temperatures are typically tropical in the lowlands along the Pacific coast and also in the far eastern region of the republic. In the coastal region, the climate fosters the growth of rubber, sugar cane, bananas, oranges, and coconut palms. To the east, though, the land is covered with dense rain forest. In the 1970s, the discovery of oil in this region created a new industry. Petroleum is now Ecuador's most important export.

Running down the middle of Ecuador are two ranges of the Andes Mountains. The tallest of the mountain peaks, at 20,000 feet above sea level, maintain snow and ice all year. Many of the mountains are volcanoes, though most have been inactive for many years. Between the two mountain ranges is a high plateau. This tableland is fertile and, consequently, supports small farming operations and small pockets of population.

As in every part of the world, Ecuador's land influences the activities that people pursue, what they grow, what they eat, and where they live. Ecuador's topography makes it easy to understand these concepts.

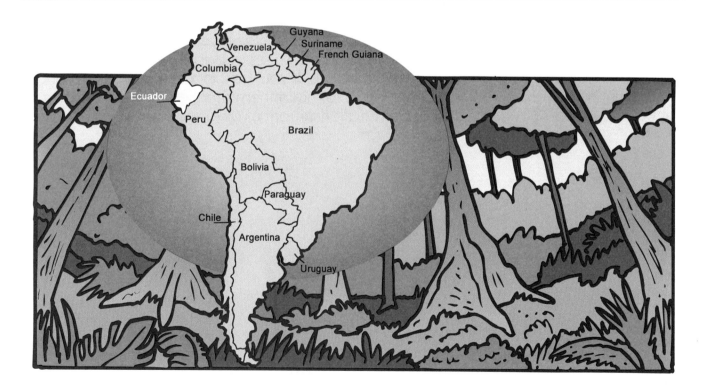

Lesson 1 Informational Writing

Here are the features of informational writing:

- It gives important information about a topic.

- It presents a main idea, which is supported with facts.

- It may include information from several different sources.

- It draws a conclusion based on the information presented.

- It is organized in a logical way. Transition words connect ideas.

When writers write to inform, they use transition words to connect ideas. **Transition words** help readers understand connections among ideas. Here are some common transition words:

again	before long	in addition
also	but	in spite of
and	consequently	therefore
as a result	finally	though
at the same time	for example	when
because	however	

Look back at Benito's report on page 98. Find the transition words that he used. Circle them.

Now, explore what you could write a report about. It is always a good idea to choose a topic in which you are interested. If you are studying regions of the world and you think Antarctica is boring, don't choose Antarctica for your topic. Instead, choose tropical rain forests or ocean life in New Zealand. To help you think of possible topics, answer these questions.

What are some places in the world that interest you or that you would like to visit?

_____ _____ _____

_____ _____ _____

What are some historical places or events that you know about? It might be an ancient city, the home of a historical figure, or the site of a famous battle.

_____ _____ _____

_____ _____ _____

Lesson 2 Facts, Opinions, and Bias

You already know what facts and opinions are. Facts can be proven to be true. Opinions are judgments that people make. What about bias?

Bias is an unfair "slant" that a writer gives to a topic. Some writers may do it by accident. Perhaps they have such strong views that they don't realize they are presenting only one point of view or only a portion of the facts. Other writers bias their work on purpose to present their own views and to persuade others to believe as they do.

Can you find the bias—the unfair slant—in this part of a report on a debate between two candidates for mayor?

> An enthusiastic crowd greeted Mr. Sam Walker and Brian O'Connor, our two candidates for mayor, at the start of the debate. Mr. Walker acknowledged his supporters, while O'Connor took his seat on stage. Mr. Walker energetically addressed each question that came his way. O'Connor took a more low-key approach as he answered questions calmly. Predictably, the questions focused on the economy and local development issues. Mr. Walker, with his background in both accounting and real estate, was well suited to handle these topics. O'Connor has a legal background.

The writer refers to one candidate, very respectfully, as "Mr. Walker." The other candidate, for whatever reason, does not get that same respect. Walker is described as "energetic," and O'Connor is only "calm." Finally, the writer provides one piece of information about the background of each candidate and implies that one man is perfectly suited to the job, while the other is not.

How could this writer have avoided bias? Consider these possibilities: He could have referred to both candidates by only their last names. He could have given equal coverage. For example, it is likely that both candidates acknowledged their supporters, so that is what should be reported. The report comments on how the candidates answered questions (energetically and calmly), but does not report on the content of the candidates' answers. How can voters judge? Can you think of other changes that would remove bias from the report?

Lesson 2 Facts, Opinions, and Bias

As a reader, it is important to recognize bias when you see it. Advertisements often include bias, which is one element of persuasion. News stories might contain bias, which could lead you to misunderstand an event or issue. It is important to think about what is fact and what is opinion and to ask whether all sides of an issue are being fairly presented. As a writer, you should ask the same questions.

Imagine that you are to write a report about the candidates Walker and O'Connor. Make up details so that your report is fair and balanced. Note the strengths and weaknesses of each man as a candidate. You may use the debate setting or another of your own choosing.

_____

_____

_____

_____

_____

_____

_____

_____

_____

_____

_____

_____

_____

_____

_____

_____

_____

_____

_____

_____

_____

_____

Lesson 3 Reliable Sources

Information is everywhere. You can get information from a book, from the Internet, from a television, or from a cell phone. Which sources of information are best? How can you tell which are good and which are not good?

First, think about the kinds of sources available. For each question, write the source that would be most useful based on the type of information required. For some questions, more than one source might be useful.

dictionary newspaper atlas	print encyclopedia online encyclopedia almanac	Web site scientific magazine

_____ On what day did Mt. St. Helens erupt?

_____ What is the migration pattern of monarch butterflies?

_____ Who won the World Series in 1978?

_____ How many acres do the Florida Everglades cover?

_____ Who recently discovered a new animal?

_____ What are Ecuador's main rivers?

_____ What is the weather forecast for tomorrow?

_____ Does *summit* have more than one meaning?

Once you find a source that seems to have the information you need, you must decide whether the source is reliable. If the source is printed, ask yourself these questions:

- **When was this source published?** If you need current information, the source should be only one or two years old. Depending on the subject, that might even be too old.

- **Who wrote this book and for what purpose?** If the book is an encyclopedia, atlas, or almanac, you can be pretty confident that responsible authors wrote it to provide information. If it is a magazine article or a work of nonfiction, you need to ask more questions. Might there be bias in the material? Is the author an expert in the field? Read the book jacket or an "About the Author" blurb in the book to discover as much as you can about the author and the purpose for writing.

Lesson 3 Reliable Sources

If you are looking at an online source, there are other questions to ask. Keep in mind that anyone can create a Web site. Just because you see information on a Web site does not mean that it is accurate.

- **What person or organization established or maintains this Web site?** What makes this person or organization an expert on the topic?

- **What is the purpose of the site?** Whether a person or an organization maintains a site, there is the potential for bias. Does the person or organization want to inform, to sell something, or to present a certain point of view (which may or may not be biased)?

- **When was the site last updated?** Just as with print sources, the publication date may matter, depending on whether you need current information.

Write *yes* or *no* to indicate whether these sources might be reliable, based on the information provided.

_____ You are writing about a South American country's economy. You refer to an encyclopedia published 6 years ago.

_____ You are writing about manatees. You refer to a Web site maintained by the Florida Department of Natural Resources.

_____ You are writing about King Tut's tomb and the artifacts found there. You refer to a Web site that includes travel logs from people who have visited the tomb.

_____ You are writing about health care in your county. You consult a report created by the country government last year that includes data about hospitals and medical providers.

Lesson 4 Taking Notes

Taking notes is what you do when you collect information for a report or presentation. Once you locate the information, your job is first to skim, to make sure the source is what you need. Then, you read carefully. Finally, you paraphrase, or briefly state in your own words, what you have read, and record it on note cards or in a writing notebook.

Here is a note card that Benito wrote when he did his research on Ecuador.

                                                    The Pacific Coast

tropical climate
fertile
grow rubber, sugar cane, bananas, oranges, coconut palms

A Guide to South America, pages 78-80

Benito's note card has three important parts. First, at the top he listed the topic. He knows that one part of his report will be about the Pacific coast, one region in Ecuador. He marks each note card with a specific topic. Labeling the cards in this way will make organizing them and writing his draft much easier.

Second, he wrote his notes. They are very brief. He did not write in complete sentences. He included only the most important pieces of information.

Finally, he wrote the name of the source and the page number. If he needs to go back and check a fact or get more information, he can do it easily.

Lesson 4 Taking Notes

Your assignment is to write a report, like Benito did, about how the land of a country affects its people. Find information about a country of your choice in a print or online source. Then, take some notes. Decide how your report will be organized and label each card with one of your main topics. Remember to keep your notes brief and to list your source at the bottom of each card. Also, remember that you must use your own words when writing, called *paraphrasing*, and not your source's words.

Lesson 5 Using an Outline

An **outline** is a way to organize information. If you are writing a report, it is an excellent step to take during your prewriting stage. After you collect information and take notes, you can outline the information to make sure you have everything you need.

Here is the outline Benito made after he completed his research on Ecuador.

Ecuador

I.   The Regions
    A. Pacific Coast
        1. typical tropical climate
        2. fertile
        3. rubber, sugar cane, bananas, oranges, coconut palms
    B. East
        1. tropical climate
        2. rainforests
        3. oil—important export since 1970s
    C. Andes Mountains
        1. two ranges run from north to south
        2. peaks to 20,000 feet
        2. snow on peaks all year
        3. fertile plateau between mountains
            a. support small farms
            b. support some population

Benito started out with his big idea: The Regions. Indented under that idea are the three regions: Pacific Coast, East, and Mountains. Under each regional heading, then, Benito listed specific, supporting details. Note that this format is called a **topic outline**. The information is recorded in short words and phrases, not in complete sentences.

Lesson 5 Using an Outline

Look back at the note cards you created on page 105. Create part of an outline from those notes. Go back to the source if you need additional information. Remember, the format and the labels look like this:

I. Main Idea

    A. Topic

        1. Supporting detail

        2. Supporting detail

_____

_____

_____

_____

_____

_____

_____

_____

_____

_____

_____

_____

_____

_____

_____

_____

_____

_____

_____

_____

_____

_____

Lesson 6 Citing Sources

The last page of a report is a **bibliography**, or an alphabetic list of sources. The bibliography shows readers what sources you used and allows them to consult those sources if they want further information. It also shows your teacher that you used a variety of sources and made good choices.

In a bibliography, you need to give certain specific information so that another person can locate that same source. Each type of source has a slightly different format. Here are examples of bibliographic entries for the most common types of sources. If, for any entry, you don't have a piece of information, just skip it and go on to the next piece of information. Pay close attention to punctuation. Periods, commas, quotation marks, and underlining are all part of the format.

Encyclopedia (print or CD-ROM)

Author (if given) last name, first name. "Title of Article." Title of Encyclopedia. Year published. Volume number, Page number.

"Ecuador." Encyclopedia Britannica. 1992. Volume 5, 360–361.

Book

Author last name, first name. Title of Book. Publisher, date of publication.

Mendoza, Carmen. Ecuador Today. Center for South American Studies, 2006.

Magazine article

Author last name, first name. "Title of Article." Title of Magazine, date of magazine: page numbers of article.

Coulon, Edouard. "South American Exports." Economy and Trade, May 7, 2006: 74–79.

Web site

Author last name, first name (if given). "Title of Article or Page." Sponsor of web site. Date of article or last update. Web site address (URL)

"Beaches, Sunshine, Sport, and the Easy Life." Ministry of Tourism, Republic of Ecuador. 2005. www.vivecuador.com

NOTE: There is no period at the end of the web site citation.

Lesson 6 Citing Sources

Now, create bibliographic entries of your own. Locate one source of each type. They don't all have to be about the same topic. What's important is that you practice using the format for each type of source.

Encyclopedia

_____

_____

_____

Book

_____

_____

_____

Magazine article

_____

_____

_____

Web site

_____

_____

_____

Lesson 7 Writing about Problems and Solutions

One way to organize a report is to use a problem-solution approach. Not all topics fit this type of format, but many do. While Benito studied Ecuador for his geography class, he learned about the problem of rain forest deforestation. For science class, he is planning a report on deforestation. Here is the problem-solution chart Benito made as part of his prewriting stage.

Problem:
Rain forests are being cut down and/or burned to create cropland.

Possible solutions:
  1. Make laws against destroying rain forests
     Enforce strong penalties
  2. Create incentives for farmers to grow plants that grow in shade
     Educate farmers about shade-loving crops
     Pay farmers to grow shade-loving crops
  3. Educate people about importance of rain forest
     Conservation
     Global warming
     Habitat to birds and animals

Recommended solution:
Educate people about the importance of the rain forest and provide incentives to prevent them from cutting and burning rain forest land.

When Benito writes his report, he will state the problem, then explore each possible solution. Finally, he will state his recommended solution and give reasons why it is the best solution to the problem.

Lesson 7 Writing about Problems and Solutions

Think of a topic that interests you. It might be an environmental issue, such as deforestation. Or it could be a local issue, such as a new housing project or a curfew law. Complete the problem-solution chart on this page.

Problem:

↓

Possible solutions:

↓

Recommended solution:

Lesson 8 The Writing Process: Informational Writing

Writing a report is one way to show what you know. It is also a way to learn about a topic that interests you. Use the writing process to plan and write a report.

Prewrite

Look back at the topic ideas you recorded on page 99. Which one seems most interesting? Choose one and begin to explore that topic with the help of this chart.

Topic: _____

What I Know	What I Want to Know	How or Where I Might Find Out

If you are comfortable with this subject, conduct research and take notes. Remember to organize your note cards by specific topic. For example, Benito organized his deforestation note cards in these categories: problem, possible solution 1, possible solution 2, possible solution 3, recommended solution.

Lesson 8 The Writing Process: Informational Writing

Now, it is time to focus on putting ideas in order. Think about your topic. How should you organize the information? By cause and effect? In order of importance? In problem-solution format? Looking at and organizing your note cards might help you decide. List your main points or ideas, in order, on this page.

Subject: _____

Method of organization: _____

Lesson 8 The Writing Process: Informational Writing

Draft

Now, write a first draft of your report. Continue on another sheet of paper if you need to. Keep your notes and the chart on page 113 nearby as you write. As you write, don't worry about misspelled words or getting everything perfect. Just get your ideas down in sentences and paragraphs.

_____

Lesson 8 The Writing Process: Informational Writing

Revise

Every writer can improve his or her work. Read your report as if you are seeing it for the first time. Remember, even experienced writers feel that revising is more difficult than writing the first draft.

Answer the questions below about your draft. If you answer "no" to any of these questions, those are the areas that might need improvement. Mark your draft, so you know what needs more work.

- Did you present information clearly and in a logical order?

- Does each paragraph consist of a main idea supported by facts?

- Did you use transition words to connect ideas?

- Did you begin with a sentence that will make readers want to keep going?

- Did you use information from several different sources?

- Did you draw a conclusion based on the information presented?

- Did you keep your audience in mind by asking yourself what they might already know or what they need to know?

- Did you present a fair and balanced view of the subject?

Here are a few pointers about making your report interesting to read.

- Vary the length of your sentences. Mixing short, medium, and long sentences keeps your readers interested.

- Vary the style of your sentences. Begin sentences with different kinds of words or clauses. For example, begin some sentences with verbs, some with phrases (such as "In a tropical rain forest,…"), and some with clauses (such as "To preserve rain forest land,…").

On page 116, write the revision of your draft. As you revise, pay special attention to the length and style of your sentences.

Lesson 8 The Writing Process: Informational Writing

_____

_____

_____

_____

_____

_____

_____

_____

_____

_____

_____

_____

_____

_____

_____

_____

_____

_____

_____

_____

_____

_____

_____

_____

_____

_____

_____

_____

_____

_____

Lesson 8 The Writing Process: Informational Writing

Proofread

Now is the time to correct those last mistakes. Proofreading is easier if you look for just one kind of error at a time. Read through once for capital letters. Read again for end punctuation. Read a third time for spelling, and so on. Use this checklist as you proofread your report.

____ Each sentence begins with a capital letter.

____ Each sentence states a complete thought and ends with the correct punctuation.

____ All proper nouns begin with capital letters.

____ All words are spelled correctly.

Use standard proofreading symbols as you proofread your revised report.

Remember to read your writing out loud during the proofreading stage. You may hear a mistake or an awkward spot that you did not see.

- <u>C</u>apitalize this letter.
- Add a missing end mark: 。 ? !
- Add a comma please.
- Fix incorrect or misspelled words.
- ~~Delete~~ this word.
- Lowercase this letter.

Publish

Write or type a final copy of your report on a separate sheet of paper. Write carefully and neatly so that there are no mistakes. Make a cover page for the front of your report. Remember to include a bibliography with your finished report. Read your report out loud to your class.

Writer's Handbook

Parts of Speech

A **noun** is a word that names a person, place, or thing. Common nouns name general things. Proper nouns name specific things and always begin with a capital letter.

Common Nouns	Proper Nouns
officer	Sergeant Rhimes
racehorse	Seattle Slew
park	Yellowstone National Park
store	Becker Hardware

A **verb** is an action word. Verbs also show a state of being. Every complete sentence has at least one verb. Verbs show action in the past, in the present, and in the future.

Last week, my team *lost*.
I *was* sad about the loss.
Today, my team *plays* against Sutherland.
Next week, we *will play* at Hinton.

An **adjective** modifies, or describes, a noun or pronoun. Adjectives tell *what kind, how much* or *how many*, or *which one*.

The *brick* building is the Community Center. *(what kind)*
It has *two* entrances. *(how many)*
I usually use *this* entrance. *(which one)*

An **adverb** modifies a verb, an adjective, or another adverb. Adverbs tell *how, when, where*, or *to what degree*.

We planned the parade *carefully*. *(how)*
We chose the date *already*. *(when)*
The parade route will go *there*. *(where)*
We are *completely* prepared. *(to what degree)*

Writer's Handbook

Punctuation

End marks on sentences show whether a sentence is a statement, a command, a question, or an exclamation.

> This sentence makes a statement.
> Make your bed, please.
> Why might you want to ask a question?
> I can't believe how excited you are!

Commas help keep ideas clear.

> In a list or series: The parade had floats, bands, and old cars.
> In a compound sentence: I waved at my dad, but I'm not sure he saw me.
> After an introductory phrase or clause: After the parade, we all had ice cream.
> To separate a speech tag: I said to Dad, "Did you see me?"

Quotation marks show the exact words that a speaker says. They enclose the speaker's words and the punctuation that goes with the words.

> "Sure, I saw you," Dad said. "How could I have missed that red hat?"
> "That's exactly why I wore it," I said.

Colons are used to introduce a series, to set off a clause, for emphasis, in time, and in business letter greetings.

> My favorite vegetables include the following: *broccoli, red peppers, and spinach.* *(series)*

> The radio announcer said: *"The game is postponed due to rain." (clause)*

> The skiers expected the worst as they got off the mountain: *an avalanche.* *(emphasis)*

Writer's Handbook

The Writing Process

When writers write, they take certain steps. Those steps make up the writing process.

Step 1: Prewrite

First, writers choose a topic. Then, they collect and organize ideas or information. They might write their ideas in a list. They might also make a chart and begin to put their ideas in some kind of order.

Tomika is going to write about her dance lessons. She put her ideas in a web.

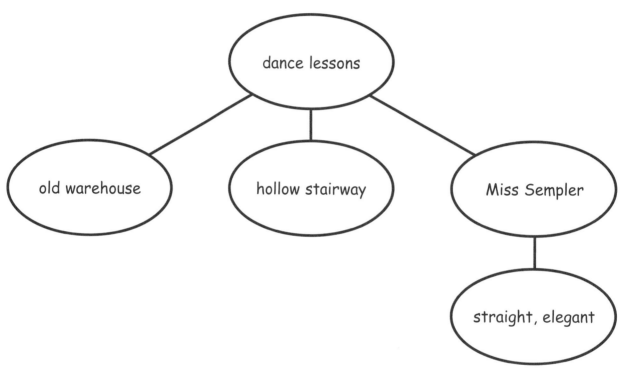

Step 2: Draft

Next, writers put their ideas on paper in a first draft. Writers know that there might be mistakes in this first draft. That's okay. Here is Tomika's first draft.

> Every Wednesday after school I eagerly climb the hollow stairway of the old Benson's Warehouse building I am glad to go dance lessons, even if they are in an old warehouse. Miss Sempler always greets the other students and me. She is so straight and elagant. She says we sound like a heard of hippoes coming up the stairs. I try to go up the stairs with my head high and my shoulders back, just like miss Sempler would.

Writer's Handbook

Step 3: Revise

Then, writers change or fix their first draft. They might decide to move ideas around or to add information. They might also take out words or sentences that don't belong. Here are Tomika's changes.

> Every Wednesday after school I eagerly climb the hollow ~~echoing~~ stairway of the old Benson's Warehouse building I am glad to go ~~to~~ dance lessons, even if they are in an old warehouse. Miss Sempler always greets the other students and me. ~~at the top of the stairs~~ She is so straight and elagant. She says we sound like a heard of hippoes coming up the stairs. I try to go up the stairs with my head high and my shoulders back, just like miss Sempler would. I almost feel like a dancer even before I get to class.

Step 4: Proofread

Writers usually write a new copy so their writing is neat. Then, they read again to make sure everything is correct. They read for mistakes in their sentences. Tomika found

> Every Wednesday after school, I eagerly climb the hollow, echoing stairway of the old Benson's Warehouse building. I am glad to go to dance lessons, even if they are in an old warehouse. Miss Sempler always greets the other students and me at the top of the stairs. She is so straight and elagant. She says we sound like a heard of hippoes coming up the stairs. I try to go up the stairs with my head high and my shoulders back, just like miss Sempler would. I almost feel like a dancer even before I get to class.

several more mistakes when she proofread her work.

Step 5: Publish

Finally, writers make a final copy that has no mistakes. They are now ready to share their writing with a reader. They might choose to read their writing out loud. They can also add pictures and create a book. There are many ways for writers to publish, or to share, their work with readers.

Writer's Handbook

Personal Narrative

In a personal narrative, a writer writes about something he has done or seen. A personal narrative can be about anything, as long as the writer is telling about one of his or her own experiences. Here is the final version of Tomika's paragraph about dance lessons.

Words that tell time indicate when something happens.

Describing words and figurative language help readers "see" or "hear" what is happening.

Every Wednesday after school, I eagerly climb the hollow, echoing stairway of the old Benson's Warehouse building. I am glad to go to dance lessons, even if they are in an old warehouse. Miss Sempler always greets the other students and me at the top of the stairs. She is so straight and elegant. She says we sound like a herd of hippos coming up the stairs. I try to go up the stairs with my head high and my shoulders back, just like Miss Sempler would. I almost feel like a dancer even before I get to class.

The words I and me show that the writer is part of the action.

The writer stayed on topic. All of the sentences give information about Tomika's dance lesson.

Descriptive Writing

When writers describe, they might tell about an object, a place, or an event. They use sensory words so that readers can see, hear, smell, feel, or taste whatever is being described. In this example of descriptive writing, Brad described the results of his science experiment.

The writer uses the whole-to-whole comparison method. He describes one plant in this paragraph, and the other plant in the next paragraph.

Daisy plant A was my control plant. It received the same amount of water as plant B, but it received no Epsom salts. Plant A has 9 leaves and is 12.5 inches tall. Its leaves are bright green, and it has a healthy appearance.

Daisy plant B received two doses of Epsom salts. The first dose was administered just as the first leaves appeared, and the second was administered one week later. Plant B has 14 leaves and is 14 inches tall. This plant also has 2 flower buds. The leaves are a deep green, and the plant is fuller and has a more pleasing appearance than does daisy plant A.

Sensory details help readers visualize the scene.

The writer gives information in the same order in each paragraph.

Writer's Handbook

Fiction Stories

Writers write about made-up things. They might write about people or animals. The story might seem real, or it might seem unreal, or fantastic. Here is a story that Jason wrote. It has human characters, and the events could really happen, so Jason's story is realistic.

The story has a beginning, a middle, and an end.	**Bitter Victory**	The first paragraph establishes the setting.

Bitter Victory

Coach had put Neil out on the field. He hadn't played all season. Neil suspected that Coach felt sorry for him, but he was glad to be in the game. Not that he figured anything would actually happen. But then, there was the ball. A Hampton player had fumbled it, and fumbled it badly. It was skittering crazily across the chewed-up grass. Now, it was coming right at him.

Neil picked up the ball and looked frantically all around him. There was a lot of confusion. Without his realizing it, Neil's feet were moving. No one was taking much notice. He crouched down a little to hide the ball tucked under his arm. He made his feet go faster and headed for the end zone. He gritted his teeth, expecting to get clobbered. Forty…thirty…twenty…ten…*Whumpf*!

A Hampton player caught him at the last moment. The impact sent Neil careening forward. He stumbled over the line, completely out of control. A sting in his ankle was quickly forgotten; Neil tasted dirt and grass as he rolled and finally came to a stop. Grinning at his approaching teammates, Neil yelled, "We won! We won!"

Neil's teammates were all yelling at him, but not about winning the game. Neil looked down at his ankle, which was bent at a nauseating angle. A blur of noises and movements occurred as Neil was loaded onto a stretcher and carried off. What he remembered, though, was the scoreboard, and the fact that the crowd went wild, just like in the movies.

Side notes:
- The story has a beginning, a middle, and an end.
- This story is written in third-person point of view. The narrator is not a part of the action. So, words such as *he, she, her, him,* and *they* refer to the characters.
- The first paragraph establishes the setting.
- Sensory words help readers visualize what is happening.
- Time and order words keep ideas clear.

Informational Writing

When writers write to inform, they present information about a topic. Informational writing is nonfiction. It is not made up; it contains facts.

Here is a paragraph from a report about the Olympics.

The Olympics

The tradition of the Olympics is a long and honorable one. The first Olympics were played in Greece more than 2,500 years ago. The initial contest was held in 776 B.C. There was just one event—a footrace. Later, the Greeks added boxing, wrestling, chariot racing, and the pentathlon. The ancient Games were held every four years for more than a thousand years.

Side notes:
- The writer states the main idea in a topic sentence. It is the first sentence of the paragraph.
- These sentences contain details that support the main idea.
- A time-order word connects ideas.

Writer's Handbook

Explanatory (or How-to) Writing

When writers explain how to do things, they might tell how to make a craft, play a computer game, or use a cell phone. Tony has written instructions for Jenna, who is going to take care of Tony's hamster while he is on vacation.

The first sentence summarizes the care instructions.

Order words help readers keep the steps in order.

Each day when you come, there are three things to do. First, check Heidi's water to make sure the bottle hasn't fallen out of place. Then, fill her food dish. Her food is in the green bag next to the cage. Finally, play with Heidi. She would love to snuggle in your neck and maybe crawl down your sleeve.

Clear words help readers understand the instructions.

Persuasive Writing

In persuasive writing, writers try to make readers think, feel, or act in a certain way. Persuasive writing shows up in newspaper and magazine articles, letters to the editor, business letters, and, of course, advertisements. Trina has written a letter to the editor of her school newsletter.

The writer begins by stating her opinion.

The writer uses an emotional appeal to persuade readers to agree with her.

Dear Editor:
    The locker bay is a mess. So many of the lockers are old, scratched, and dented. Some of them don't even close properly. How can we be proud of our school when the locker room is falling apart? More importantly, the worn-out lockers seem to encourage students to mistreat them even further. Someone needs to repair or replace the lockers so that we can feel good about our school.
Trina Hardesty

The writer states facts to lend support to her opinions.

The writer includes a specific request for action.

Writer's Handbook

Business Letters

Writers write business letters to people or organizations with whom they are not familiar. Business letters usually involve a complaint or a request for information. Mariko needs information for a school report. She wrote a business letter to request information.

The heading includes the sender's address and the date.	8213 Rivera Boulevard Fredericksburg, TX 78624 March 4, 2008
The inside address is the complete name and address of the recipient.	Dr. Olivia Lamas, DVM Lamas Animal Clinic 944 Curry Lane Fredericksburg, TX 78624

Dear Dr. Lamas: ← **A colon follows the greeting.**

My class is exploring careers this month. I would like to learn about being a veterinarian. Is there a time when I can visit your office? I have many questions, and I would like to watch you work with the animals.

Please call my teacher, Ms. Zapata, to set up a time that is convenient for you. The school's phone number is 830-555-0021.

Thank you for your help, and I look forward to meeting you.

The text of the letter is the body.

Sincerely, ← **A comma follows the closing.**

Mariko Campillo
Mariko Campillo

The sender always includes a signature.

Answer Key

Chapter 1

Lesson 1

Page 5
Topic sentence: The bluebirds playing in my yard are a lovely sight.
Possible details:
Their bright features easily catch my eye. They appear in groups of two or three. They move about in a lively way. The little chitter almost sounds like laughter.

Page 6
Possible main idea: Birds can be annoying.
Paragraphs will vary.

Lesson 2

Page 7
Underlined topic sentence: When I was a kid, I especially loved stories that had animals as characters.
Crossed-out sentence: The mice in our attic sometimes make noise at night.
Paragraphs will vary.

Lesson 3

Page 9
Order of steps shown:
Step 2: Draft
Step 5: Publish
Step 3: Revise
Step 1: Prewrite
Step 4: Proofread

Lesson 4

Page 10
Yes, because Mrs. Prescott used words that adults would understand. She also provided information that parents would want to know.

Page 11
Suggestions may include the time of the field trip, how children will be transported, who will be supervising parents, how children should dress, whether parents are invited or allowed to attend, whether children need a sack lunch, and so on.
Information sheets for students will vary.

Lesson 5

Page 12
Details will vary.
Paragraphs will vary.

Page 13
Revised, proofread, and rewritten paragraphs will vary.

Answer Key

Chapter 2

Lesson 1

Page 15
Responses to idea-starters will vary.

Lesson 2

Page 16
Time words and phrases will vary.
Sentences will vary.

Page 17
Circled words in paragraph: *After, after, supper, tomorrow*
Paragraphs will vary.

Lesson 3

Page 19
Students should notice that the paragraph that uses passive voice is longer than the paragraph that uses active voice.
<u>Nick</u> was watching the storm.
X The <u>sky</u> was lit up by lightning.
X The <u>yard</u> was littered with branches.
<u>Pete</u> was amazed.
Sentences will vary.

Lesson 4

Page 20
Ideas and idea webs will vary.

Page 21
Entries in sequence charts will vary.

Page 22
Drafts will vary.

Page 24
Revisions will vary.

Answer Key

Chapter 3

Lesson 1

Page 26
Possible details:
See: groceries on one side, neon signs hang from the ceiling, yellow wastebasket, tall glass
Hear: whining, whirring, back-up beeps
Smell: spicy scent
Touch: tall, cold glass
Taste: grilled chicken, sweet iced tea

Page 27
Details and paragraphs will vary.

Lesson 2

Page 28
Sentences will vary.

Page 29
Possible revised sentences:
A tuba player clumsily dropped his tuba.
The flag-bearers waved their flags energetically.
Marching in a long parade can be very tiring.
Carrying a bass drum must be extremely hard.
The crowd always loves the high school band.

Lesson 3

Page 30
Circled spatial words: *into, forward, middle, left, Inside, right, far end*
Paragraphs will vary.

Page 31
Descriptive paragraphs will vary.

Lesson 4

Page 32
Details and paragraphs will vary.

Page 33
Details and paragraphs will vary.

Lesson 5

Page 34
The alligator is bigger than the rabbit.
If you touch the rabbit, it will surely be softer than the alligator.
The alligator's skin would be much more scaly than the rabbit's.
It would be more dangerous to meet an alligator than to meet a rabbit.

Page 35
Comparative sentences will vary.
Comparative forms used should be *most energetic, highest, messiest, tamest.*

Lesson 6

Page 36
Entries in Venn diagrams will vary.

Page 37
Paragraphs will vary.

Lesson 7

Page 38
Entries in Venn diagrams will vary.

Page 39
Comparisons will vary.

Lesson 8

Page 40
Topic ideas will vary.
Entries in idea webs will vary.

Page 41
Methods of organization and paragraphs will vary.

Page 42
Revisions will vary.

Page 43
Published descriptive paragraphs will vary.

Answer Key

Chapter 4

Lesson 1

Page 46

Narrator: the "I"; a name is not given

Main character: the narrator

Possible details: He is "normal." Lives in Iowa by Mississippi River. Lives in small town. Parents are "normal."

Details revealed: through narrator

Other characters: Mom—cashier at grocery store, Dad—mechanic, Jeremiah—"interesting," not normal

Setting: in small town in Iowa

Possible problem: There could be some conflict with Jeremiah and the main character or between Jeremiah and the character's parents.

Dialogue (possible answers):

Main character: He has good manners—says "please."

Other character: He does not speak.

Sensory details: board games, homemade bread, green beans, red radishes, galvanized pails, brown egg, brown eyes, neatest printing

Lesson 2

Page 47

Iowa, Mississippi River, Wisconsin across river, the town is small (has only one grocery store)

Page 48

Information from passage: Cotton fields and woods are in view; setting must be in country. Mississippi.

Sensory details: draped in a cloak of gray mist; sun chased the night; glisten greenly; jackets of emerald and gold; dark, almost black; soft breeze; voices whispered

Mood or feeling (possible responses): The mood is serious, but hopeful.

Words that convey mood: quietness, empty

Responses will vary.

Page 49

Responses and paragraphs will vary.

Lesson 3

Page 50

Characters listed will vary.

"My Normal Life" character details (possible answers):

Character is a kid—the narrator refers to parents

Character lives in Iowa—narrator reveals information

Character hasn't traveled much—narrator reveals information

Dad is a mechanic—narrator reveals information

Mom is a clerk in a grocery store—narrator reveals information

Characters live in a small town—narrator reveals that the town has only one grocery store

Page 51

Responses and paragraphs will vary.

Lesson 4

Page 52

Responses will vary.

Page 53

"Who is Jeremiah?" I asked.

She smiled suddenly and said, "I went to grade school with him."

"So, he's been around here, all these years?" I quizzed.

Dialogue will vary.

Chapter 4 continued

Lesson 5

Page 55
Responses will vary.

Lesson 6

Page 56
Responses will vary.
Realistic story ideas will vary.

Page 57
Responses will vary.
Fantasy story ideas will vary.

Lesson 7

Page 58
Character details in idea webs will vary.

Page 59
Story maps will vary.

Page 60
Drafts will vary.

Page 62
Revisions will vary.

Chapter 5

Lesson 1

Page 65
Persuasive statements will vary.

Lesson 2

Page 66
Circled opinion signal words (instructions on page 70): *should, think, think*

Page 67
Possible facts from Daniel's article:
Reading is important.; Students at WRMS don't have access to library.; Library is closed before and after school.; There is no time to go to library between classes.
Possible opinions from Daniel's article:
School should rethink the library and its use; Students are more likely to be motivated if they choose their own reading material.
Fact from Juanita's paragraph:
She knows kids who don't know what's in the library.; There is so much information out there.
Circled opinion signal words: *think, should, should*
Possible opinions from Juanita's paragraph:
We should take Daniel's idea further.; School should offer a research class.
Students' personal opinions will vary.

Lesson 3

Page 68
Issues will vary.

Answer Key

Chapter 5 continued

Page 69

The emotional appeal in Ms. Tavenor's letter is aimed at strong feelings that people have about education and their children. It also gets at strong feelings people have about how their tax dollars are spent.

Letters to the editor will vary.

Lesson 4

Page 70

The ad wants to make readers feel comfortable, just as if they were eating at home with their family.

You "need" one of these if you are a sports fan.

Audience for action movie: teens and adults.

Writers would need to appeal to strong feelings of action and drama.

Page 71

Slogans and advertisements will vary.

Lesson 5

Page 72

Reasons why the school should contribute to the Literacy Board's project:

1) To prepare children for reading, the Literacy Board will distribute books to youngsters as young as 1 year old.
2) The Literacy Board is a non-profit organization and needs our help for this important project.
3) For every dollar our school contributes to "Ready to Read," the Board will distribute four books.
4) Providing books to families with young children will encourage parents to read with their children.
5) Children who are read to at home are far more likely to be ready to read when they enter kindergarten.
6) <u>Studies show that students who enter school ready to read are likely to have more successful school careers than students who are not "reading ready" upon kindergarten entry.</u>

Page 73

Prewriting notes and ideas will vary.

Lesson 6

Page 75

Persuasive articles will vary.

Lesson 7

Page 76

Students' ideas will vary.
Entries in idea webs will vary.

Page 77

Students' organizational notes will vary.

Page 78

Drafts will vary.

Page 80

Revisions will vary.

Answer Key

Chapter 6

Lesson 1

Page 82
Responses will vary.

Page 83
Order words underlined in paragraph:
First, Then, Finally
Responses will vary.

Lesson 2

Page 84
Possible causes and effects:
Cause: Oil choked out vegetation. Effect: Fish and amphibians died.
Cause: Citizens cleaned up. Effect: River is nearly healthy again.

Page 85
Possible causes and effects:
Cause: The aunt and uncle are cruel. Effect: The boys run away.
Cause: The boys go to Venice. Effect: They meet the Thief Lord.
Cause: The Thief Lord offers food and shelter. Effect: The boys are grateful.
Cause: A mysterious turn of events occurs. Effect: The children are in danger.
Responses will vary.

Lesson 3

Page 86
Circled words in paragraph: *result, Because, so*
Possible causes and effects:
Cause: A person made a 9-1-1 call. Effect: The fire department made a run.
Cause: The caller had seen smoke. Effect: He called 9-1-1.
Cause: The caller had acted quickly. Effect: Firefighters saved the structure.
Cause: An electric heater had faulty wiring. Effect: The heater was the cause of the fire.

Page 87
Responses will vary.
Paragraphs will vary.

Lesson 4
Page 88
Tables should be similar to this:

Bus Stop 40		
6:37 a.m.	16A	to Clayton College
6:48 a.m.	2A	to north
7:01 a.m.	44D	to College Mall
7:12 a.m.	24C	to downtown
7:28 a.m.	7A	to Clayton College

Page 89
Visual aids will vary.

Lesson 5

Page 90
Underlined words in paragraph: *First, west, past, down, right, right, after, turn, right, up, beyond*

Page 91
Directions will vary.

Lesson 6

Page 92
Responses and entries in idea webs will vary.

Page 93
Entries in organizational chart will vary.

Page 94
Instructions will vary.

Page 96
Revisions will vary.

Answer Key

Chapter 7

Lesson 1

Page 98
Circled transition words (instructions on page 99): *But, also, and, though, now, and, consequently, and*

Page 99
Topic explorations will vary.

Lesson 2

Page 101
Reports will vary.

Lesson 3

Page 102
print encyclopedia; web site; almanac
web site; online encyclopedia
almanac; print encyclopedia
web site; online encyclopedia
scientific magazine
atlas
newspaper
dictionary

Page 103
no
yes
no
yes

Lesson 4

Page 105
Entries on note cards will vary.

Lesson 5

Page 107
Outlines will vary.

Lesson 6

Page 109
Bibliographic entries will vary, but must follow the formats given.

Lesson 7

Page 111
Entries in chart will vary.

Lesson 8

Page 112
Entries in chart will vary.

Page 113
Entries in chart will vary.

Page 114
Drafts will vary.

Page 116
Revisions will vary.

Notes

Notes

Notes